THE BOOK

The Book

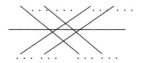

STÉPHANE MALLARMÉ

TRANSLATED & WITH AN INTRODUCTION BY

SYLVIA GORELICK

EXACT CHANGE

CAMBRIDGE

2018

• • •

TRANSLATOR'S INTRODUCTION

*

BY SYLVIA GORELICK

"Everything in the world exists to end up as a book."
—Stéphane Mallarmé, "The Book: Spiritual Instrument"[1]

In his essay "The Book to Come," Maurice Blanchot draws attention to the highly contingent nature of the notes which, in 1957, Jacques Scherer published under the title *Le "Livre" de Mallarmé*. Mallarmé had ordered, in a note written near the end of his life, that all his papers be burned after his death: "Burn, then: there is no literary inheritance there, my poor children."[2] He further instructed that no one should be given access to his papers. This mandate was first broken with their exposure to Paul Valéry several days after the poet's death in 1898. Now what we have under the title *The Book* is a collection of notes whose exact intended purpose remains obscure. It is the fragmented manifestation of what, from 1866 onward, the poet had spoken of as the Book (*Livre*) or Work (*Oeuvre*), the impossible and necessary culmination of his poetic practice. On this point, Blanchot criticizes the presupposition of unity involved in Scherer's publication of these notes under the aegis of the name *Le Livre*. In this line of thinking, there is an argument against publishing, republishing, and translating the manuscripts that comprise the unfinished work. Yet it seems clear that this complex text presents Mallarmé's idea of the Book made material. The Book

---

[1] Stéphane Mallarmé, "Le Livre, instrument spirituel," *Igitur - Divagations - Un coup de dès*, ed. Bertrand Marchal (Paris: Gallimard, 2003), 274. Translations are my own unless otherwise noted.

[2] Stéphane Mallarmé, letter to Marie and Geneviève Mallarmé, September 8, 1898, in Stéphane Mallarmé, *Oeuvres complètes I*, ed. Bertrand Marchal (Paris: Gallimard, "Bibliothèque de la Pléiade" collection, 1998), 821. Translation by Charlotte Mandell in Maurice Blanchot, *The Book to Come* (Stanford: Stanford University Press, 2003), 265.

as idea was marked, for the poet, by its unrealizability. For the very reason that the manuscripts cannot actualize this idea, they represent an invaluable resource for understanding Mallarmé's thought and his poetics.

The manuscripts for *The Book* comprise over 200 pages of notes dating from the last decade of Mallarmé's life. These pages contain poetry, theoretical writing, drafts of letters, symbolic diagrams, and meticulous mathematical calculations for the printing of the text and its theatrical presentation in a series of organized sessions (*séances*) in which the audience, partially chosen and partially aleatory, was to participate. These pages also contain large sections of text that were crossed out and replaced with others—their spatial organization is both precise and nonlinear. Like the sessions that they envision and plan out, the pages of the manuscripts themselves proceed according to the logic, at once luminous and hidden, of an intricate staging.

In 1897, Mallarmé published *Divagations*, which includes a collection of writings titled "Scribbled at the Theater." Here, Mallarmé traces a theatrics that is linked to poetry. In the piece "Of Genre and the Moderns" he writes: "Theater is, by essence, superior...No poet could think himself foreign to such objectivity of the play of the soul."[3] He further claims that poetry seals the group of "diverse arts" whose task it is to provide "a religious or official character" to "[the] stage, our only magnificence."[4] Such a religiosity is needed, Mallarmé claims, in order to "fashion divinity."[5] The goal of theater is thus presented as the conjuration of a divine presence, effected through the force of poetry. The short piece "Mimique," which focuses on a performance by the mime Paul Margeuritte, advances an act of *mimesis* as the mode in which the mime's theatrical self-presentation takes place. Through this mimetic act, "[the] stage illustrates...the idea,"[6] giving it presence only through a veil of falsity. The poet's role is here designated as that of translating the silence of this gesture. Read in conjunction with these writings, *The Book* presents the continuation of such a theatrical thinking. However, here this theatrics is poised for enactment. I wish to suggest that

---

[3] Stéphane Mallarmé, "Of Genre and the Moderns," *Divagations*, trans. Barbara Johnson (Cambridge: Harvard University Press, 2009), 142.

[4] Mallarmé, "Of Genre and the Moderns," *Divagations*, 143.

[5] Mallarmé, "Of Genre and the Moderns," *Divagations*, 143. Translation modified.

[6] Mallarmé, "Mimique," *Divagations*, 140.

the specificity of this unfinished text lies in its unique relationship to performance.

*

A letter of 1866 marks the genesis of Mallarmé's dream of the Book.[7] This idea comes with a revelation of the groundlessness of existence and the absence of ideality, resulting in a radical materialism. Mallarmé's letter was written relatively early in his poetic career. In 1865, he had presented the first version of *The Afternoon of a Faun* to Banville and Coquelin, who had turned it down for the Théâtre-Français and in 1867, he would publish *Hérodiade*. Mallarmé writes to Henri Cazalis:

> Yes, *I know it*, we are nothing but vain forms of matter—but sublime indeed to have invented God and our soul…I want to give myself this spectacle of matter, in full awareness of it, and yet, soaring fervently into the Dream that it knows it is not, singing the Soul and all the other divine impressions that have amassed in us since the earliest times, and proclaiming these glorious lies before the Nothingness that is truth! Such is the plan of my Lyric volume, and perhaps this will be its title, *The Glory of the Lie*, or *The Glorious Lie*.[8]

Poetry, with its privileged relationship to mendacity, represents a source of power in the face of materiality. Without a divine substratum for thought, Mallarmé suggests, we can nonetheless hope for a book in which the "spectacle of matter" and the dream of idealism would be synthesized.

From this point forward, Mallarmé holds this project as a goal, which he will pursue, redefine, and continue throughout his life. A year later, he refers to it as "*the Work*, the Great Work as our ancestors, the alchemists, said."[9] He then speaks of his Work, "as it is dreamed of," as the third "great

---

[7] In this genealogy of the idea of the Book, I am indebted to Bertrand Marchal's "Notice" on the unfinished manuscript, published as *Notes en vue du "Livre"* in the 1998 Pléiade edition of Mallarmé's complete works (*Oeuvres complètes I*, 1372–1383).

[8] Mallarmé, letter to Henri Cazalis, April 28, 1866, *Oeuvres complètes I*, 696.

[9] Mallarmé, letter to Cazalis, May 14 or 17, 1867, *Oeuvres complètes I*, 715.

scintillation of Beauty on this earth" after the Venus de Milo and da Vinci's *Mona Lisa*.[10] Yet, before this project, he finds himself overcome with a feeling of powerlessness and despair. In April 1868, he writes to François Coppée, saying: "It has now been two years since I committed the sin of seeing the Dream in its ideal nudity while I should have amassed a mystery of music and forgetfulness between it and myself. And now that I've arrived at the horrible vision of a pure Work, I've nearly lost my mind and the meaning of the most familiar words."[11] The blinding light that this idea of the Book radiates comes from the realization that there is no nudity of truth to be arrived at. Rather, any tearing of the veil of beauty can only result in a fall into a chasm, where all things are irreducibly veiled. To this state of affairs, Mallarmé responds with a simultaneous recoiling before the impossibility of his project and a wild leap into the future.

A turn takes place in 1869–70, during which the poet seeks "the scientific foundation" of what he calls "the work of my heart and my solitude."[12] In 1871, the Book takes the form of a multivolume opus, in which each tome will represent a different mode of inquiry and literary genre. He writes to Cazalis: "My work is no longer a myth. (A volume of Tales, dreamed. A volume of Poetry, glimpsed and crooned. A volume of Criticism, be it what was once called the Universe, considered from a strictly *literary* point of view.) In short, the mornings of twenty years."[13] The Book here appears as a realizable idea—a lifework that it will take two decades to compose. Yet this concept will undergo a metamorphosis.

The idea of the Book disappears from archival view for fifteen years, during which time Mallarmé's literary renown is significantly established. In this period, he publishes the poem "Funeral Toast" for Théophile Gautier (1873), his translation of Edgar Allan Poe's *The Raven*, illustrated by Édouard Manet (1875), the final version of *The Afternoon of a Faun*, also illustrated by Manet (1876), his language textbook *English Words* (1878), and his translation of George W. Cox's *A Manual of Mythology* under the title *The Ancient Gods* (*Les Dieux antiques*) (1880). In 1884, Paul Verlaine published *The Cursed Poets*, dedicated to Mallarmé, Arthur Rimbaud, and Tristan Corbière,

---

[10] Mallarmé, letter to Eugène Lefébure, May 27, 1867, *Oeuvres complètes I*, 717.

[11] Mallarmé, letter to François Coppée, April 20, 1868, *Oeuvres complètes I*, 726-7.

[12] Mallarmé, letter to Lefébure, March 20, 1870, *Oeuvres complètes I*, 751–2.

[13] Mallarmé, letter to Cazalis, March 3, 1871, *Oeuvres complètes I*, 759.

while Joris-Karl Huysmans published *Against the Grain*, which included admiring quotations of Mallarmé's poetry. These two works further solidified the poet's status in the literary world. In November 1885, Mallarmé writes a letter to Verlaine in which the mythic idea of the Book reemerges and takes a new shape, which no longer corresponds to a material form, but of which any manifestation would necessarily fall short as an approximation—it constitutes the unreachable "limit of universal literature."[14] In this letter, sent in response to Verlaine's request for material to be used in a biography of Mallarmé for the journal *Les Hommes d'aujourhd'hui*, which would be published two years later, the poet presents the following idea:

> The Book, convinced that at bottom there is only one, attempted unknowingly by all those who have written, even Geniuses. The Orphic explanation of the Earth, which is the only duty of the poet and the literary game *par excellence*: for the very rhythm of the book, at once impersonal and alive, down to its pagination, is juxtaposed to the equations of this dream, or Ode.
>
> This is the avowal of my vice exposed, dear friend, which I've rejected a thousand times, my spirit scarred or weary, but I am possessed by it and I will succeed perhaps—not in producing this work in its entirety (I don't know who one would have to be to do that!) but to show a fragment of it completed, to make its glorious authenticity flicker from one position, indicating the totality of the rest for which a life is not enough.[15]

In this way, the dream of the Book is reformulated under the sign of a totality that is both in the process of becoming and deferred to a future beyond the limits of "a life"—beyond the measure of a merely human temporality. In "Crisis of Verse," Mallarmé presents the notion of the Book in terms of an ideal Bible, writing that "there would only be one [book] in the world—its law—a Bible of the kind that nations simulate."[16] Such an Ur-text of being can only, Mallarmé suggests, occur as a simulation. This

---

[14] Marchal, "Notice" in Mallarmé, *Oeuvres complètes I*, 1375.

[15] Mallarmé, letter to Paul Verlaine, Novemeber 16, 1885, *Oeuvres complètes I*, 788.

[16] Mallarmé, "Crise de vers," *Igitur - Divagations - Un coup de dès*, 257.

reaching back to an origin point of humanity in the form of a Book has the effect of a delay, pushing this ideal origin into an unknowable futurity. Such a relay between past and future takes place as a work of *mimesis*. It does not occur—it never can and never will—and thus it must take place as a self-conscious simulacrum within the theater of literature. The mimetic shadow-play of Mallarmé's practice keeps close to the idealism it imitates—aware that ideal foundations are absent, it proceeds within the element of a radical materiality, conjuring an image of the divine. The Book thus entails what Jean Hyppolite calls Mallarmé's "materialism of the idea."[17]

Following this semi-public letter to Verlaine, Mallarmé will become, in Marchal's words, "the poet of the Book *par excellence*" for the symbolist poets.[18] In 1895 he writes an article titled "The Book: Spiritual Instrument" for *La Revue Blanche*, which begins as follows: "A proposition that emanates from me—cited diversely in praise or blame—I claim it along with those that follow here—says, in brief, that everything in the world exists to end up as a book."[19] While this could be read as a totalizing desire to reduce life to literature, its meaning should be seen through the evolution of the Book as idea. In this light, the proposition means that earthly life projects its own dream of itself as a totality into the future, which can only be realized in pieces—materially, in ink and pages.

Like *The Book*, Mallarmé's *A Throw of the Dice Will Never Abolish Chance* (1897) is centered on the relation between ideality and materiality; in this work, what the poet calls the "prismatic subdivisions of the Idea" are typographically organized on the page in a precisely calculated "spiritual *mise en scène*."[20] While there are multiple resonances between the two works,

---

[17] Hyppolite identifies this principle at work in Mallarmé's *A Throw of the Dice*, writing: "within this materialism of the idea he imagines the diverse possibilities for reading the text" (Jean Hyppolite, "Le coup de dés de Stéphane Mallarmé et le message," *Les Etudes philosophiques*, 1958, no. 4. Cited in Jacques Derrida, "The Double Session," *Dissemination*, trans. Barbara Johnson (London: The Athlone Press, 1981), 207).

[18] Marchal, "Notice" in Mallarmé, *Oeuvres complètes I*, 1375.

[19] Mallarmé, "Le Livre, instrument spirituel," *Igitur - Divagations - Un coup de dès*, 274.

[20] Mallarmé, "Préface de l'édition *Cosmopolis*" of *Un Coup de Dés*, *Igitur - Divagations - Un coup de dès*, 442.

there are also marked differences. Richard Sieburth has noted that if *A Throw of the Dice* evidences Mallarmé's preoccupation with the typographical disposition of the printed page, the meticulous manuscripts for *The Book* bear witness to the poet's strong investment and participation in "a fin-de-siècle manuscript culture still based on the handwritten—and auratic—transmission of text."[21] Mallarmé's concern, in *A Throw of the Dice*, with the rigorous spatialization of words on the page into a "constellation"[22] certainly persists in *The Book*. Yet here, this spatiality expands beyond the symbolic space of the page and into urban space—while the text opens onto the street in the first page of the manuscripts, Mallarmé invokes such a space in other ways—at one point, for example, he writes: "more city of the future poet."[23] Moreover, *The Book*, unlike *A Throw of the Dice*, points to its own realization in a series of performances.

*

In the pages of *The Book*, the event of its theatrical presentation is discussed in terms of an *operation*, which takes different forms. In one instance, the operation is defined as the process by which "[the] Hero extracts the Hymn from the [Drama]."[24] In another, a "pure / financial operation"[25] is designated. To shed some light on the mode of this poetic operation, I would like to turn to two readings of Mallarmé; first, Blanchot's reflections on Mallarméan temporality in "The Book to Come" and second, Jacques Derrida's thinking of Mallarmé's concept of *mimesis* in "The Double Session."

In "The Book to Come" Blanchot claims that the temporality of Mallarmé's writing has one dimension of fixity and one of profound disjunction: "His work is sometimes fixed in a white, immobile virtuality; sometimes...animated by an extreme temporal discontinuity."[26] Beneath the play between these two temporal modes, Blanchot writes, the "time

---

[21] Richard Sieburth, "MS Fr 270: Prelude to a Translation," *L'Esprit Créateur*, Vol. XL, No. 3 (Fall 2000), 97–107, 99.
[22] See Mallarmé's letter to André Gide of May 14, 1897, *Oeuvres complètes I*, 816.
[23] Mallarmé, *The Book* (Cambridge: Exact Change, 2018), 29.
[24] Mallarmé, *The Book*, 180.
[25] Mallarmé, *The Book*, 157.
[26] Blanchot, *The Book to Come*, 230.

expressed by the work" takes place, which is "a time without present." [27] Indeed, in "Restrained Action," Mallarmé writes, "there is no Present, no—a present does not exist."[28] In "Mimique" he writes, "here anticipating, there recalling, in the future, in the past, *under the false appearance of a present.*"[29] It is because of this impossibility of presence that, as Blanchot says, "the Book must never be regarded as being truly there."[30] Rather, it is always deferred to the irreality of a future or situated in the irreality of a past. The present fabricated by the material idea of The Book incessantly divides and flies off in these two dimensionless directions. This temporal structure is present in the notes of *The Book*:

> All we know is that she [...]
> lies in the tenebrous past —
> indeed the desert took her back —
> unless she lies in
> the future —[31]

And yet the present must be conjured for the work to take place, and this conjuration must happen theatrically. This relationship to a fictive presence is referred to in the near-axiomatic phrase:

> a book neither begins nor ends: at most it
> pretends[32]

This performance of presence plays out through what Mallarmé calls, at one point, "an operation called Poetry."[33] *The Book*'s operation thus gains a certain clarity; as a temporal event, it proceeds between the constant division of moments into past and future—it only properly *occurs* through a fabrication, a prosthesis of presence.

---

[27] Blanchot, *The Book to Come*, 230.

[28] Mallarmé, "L'Action restreinte," *Igitur - Divagations - Un coup de dès*, 265.

[29] Mallarmé, "Mimesis," *Divagations*, 140.

[30] Blanchot, *The Book to Come*, 230.

[31] Mallarmé, *The Book*, 29–30.

[32] Mallarmé, *The Book*, 204.

[33] Mallarmé, *The Book*, 116.

In "The Double Session," Derrida conceives Mallarméan *mimesis* as "a double that doubles no simple, a double that nothing anticipates, nothing at least that is not itself already double." The form that results, he writes, is "a ghost that is the phantom of no flesh."[34] In this perspective, Mallarmé's temporal and mimetic operation evacuates ontology from language. Instead of referring back to an origin, his poetics imitates nothing or Nothingness, moving outside the possibility of presence. Likewise, in *The Book*, the performative repetition of the word "Idea" proceeds as an obsessive emptying of this term of any Platonic concept that would inscribe it as an originary *eidos*—as a principle in which truth could be unveiled. Through his mimetic process, Mallarmé exposes the essentially veiled nature of truth.[35] This double—the Platonic simulacrum as a *copy of a copy* displaced beyond reference to an original idea—has its reverberations in *The Book*'s text:

> This is all the echo says —
> double and lying, interrogated
> by the voyaging spirit (wind)[36]

Derrida focuses his analysis on "Mimique"—here, Mallarmé sets out a poetic program constructed around the art of the mime. The task of poetry is framed as that of a pantomime, emptied of any possible referent, that shapes space, marks boundaries, and opens possibilities. It is explicitly within the stage—the theatrical framework whose scaffolding *The Book* is always

---

[34] Derrida, *Dissemination*, 206.

[35] Here I am diverging from both Derrida and Marchal's interpretations of Mallarmé's poetics, which each privilege the concept of the undecidable rupture of the veil as a violation of virginity. Derrida thematizes the concept of the "hymen" as the "(pure and impure) difference" that appears in the work (or "hymn") to dislocate the present, and which is never either broken or not broken (Derrida, *Dissemination*, 210). Marchal, for his part, reinterprets a recurring word in Mallarmé's manuscript as *pucel* (virgin), which he works into his interpretation in order to stage the following problematic within *The Book*: "unveil the Idea or re-veil it; eat the woman or die of hunger (*manger la dame, ou mourir de faim*)" (Mallarmé, *Oeuvres complètes I*, 1383). Based on a close analysis of Mallarmé's handwriting, I have determined that the word Marchal interprets as *pucel* is in fact *fusil* (gun)—a term that appears frequently in the text.

[36] Mallarmé, *The Book*, 29.

working on, taking apart, and reconfiguring—that this simulation of presence and of ideality takes place. In this respect, the performative aspect of the text is central—indeed, this text develops, in a certain sense, as a performance score. For its enactment, it was necessary that the text of *The Book* to be performed possess the quality of mobility—that it be open to a multitude of permutations: "the manuscript alone / is mobile —."[37]

Indeed, Mallarmé thought of literature and theater as inseparable—a unity that culminates in the manuscripts for *The Book*. In a letter to Vittorio Pica, he wrote: "I believe that Literature, taken at its source which is Art and Science, will give rise to a Theater for us, where the performances will be the true modern religion; a Book, an explanation of man sufficient to our most beautiful dreams."[38] And in the pages of *The Book*, he writes:

> identity of the
> Book and the Play[39]

I would like to suggest that it is precisely in terms of this theatricality that the unfinished and unfinishable nature of The Book is manifested. In its performative mode, the text both enacts and defers the enactment of the idea of the Book. It is constitutively fragmentary, self-destructive, and mobile—in the process of its writing and in its future realization. In this sense, the manuscripts that compose *The Book* constitute, in a significant respect, the precise material realization of the idea that preoccupied Mallarmé for over thirty years. They show a material ideality that has not yet had its time—they communicate an injunction to the reader-participant to theatrically fabricate a present in which it could take place.

*

This translation is dedicated to Lizzy McDaniel, who breathed life and song into Mallarmé's unfinished writings. With endless love in our poetic *association terrestre* and beyond.

---

[37] Mallarmé, *The Book*, 61.
[38] Mallarmé, letter to Vittorio Pica, December 1886 or January 1887 (*Correspondances* III, 83, cited in *Oeuvres complètes I*, 1376).
[39] Mallarmé, *The Book*, 144.

NOTE ON THE TEXT

The manuscripts for *The Book*, held in Harvard's Houghton Library and accessible in digital facsimile, are enigmatic—difficult not only to translate but to decipher, to read. They have a hermetic aspect, folding in upon themselves indefinitely. A great many lines of these pages were crossed out by Mallarmé. While Scherer's 1957 transcription of the manuscript renders these crossed-out sections as footnotes and Marchal's version in the 1998 *Pléiade* edition underlines these sections, I have rendered them as literally crossed out, so that they appear in these pages in a way directly analogous to the handwritten pages themselves. Following Marchal's lead, however, I have set the blocks of text through which multiple diagonal lines are traced in italics. Words and phrases underlined in the manuscript have been underlined here as well. In this translation, words appearing in smaller type above or below crossed-out sections of text represent the replacements of omitted phrases. Rather than erring on the side of continuity, as Scherer does with his use of footnotes, and as Marchal does by collapsing spatial distances within the page, I have maintained, to the best of my ability, a radical fidelity to the visual and spatial organization of Mallarmé's manuscripts. I have endeavored to communicate, in this translation, the profound discontinuity of the text—the relationship it has to its own obsessive revision and refashioning—its internal disjunction.

I have translated *The Book* referring to Mallarmé's original manuscript. While I have most often followed the guidelines of Marchal's transcription in my translation, and at times of Scherer's, there are words and phrases that I have reinterpreted and translated based on a close study of the manuscript pages, and of Mallarmé's handwriting. My handwriting analysis proceeded through the careful process of following patterns in the poet's script—tracking the range of appearances of letters, and taking these variations and limits into account in each case of unclarity.

The recurring word *feuille* I have translated as *leaf*, which is distinguished, in the manuscript, from *page*. The leaf should be considered as a folio, a single sheet of paper in a book, while the page is the full space of the paper folded into leaves. I have chosen to translate the word *représentation* as *performance* and *interprétation* as *interpretation*. While *interprétation* can equally signify "reading" or "performance" I found it important to maintain its stability in the concept of the interpretive, and to distinguish it from the terms *lecture* (reading) and *représentation* (performance), which appear frequently in the text. I have translated the often-repeated word *soit* as "be it"—this phrase has the double function of acting as a mathematical term to designate what is given, and possesses an incantatory value, as in the uttering of a prayer. The word *séance*, which plays an important role in *The Book*, has been rendered as "session," in accordance with its most general signification. I have reproduced, here, the archival pagination of the manuscripts, written directly on the pages themselves, which is included in both Scherer and Marchal's editions.

There are a number of symbolic figures that circulate in the manuscript of *The Book*. These include *Theater* (often abbreviated as "Th"), *Mystery* (often abbreviated as "Myst"), *Drama* (often abbreviated as "Dr"), *Hero*, *Hymn*, and *Idea*. They appear in various permutations of diagrams and calculations which are both mirrored by and combined with the precise calculations for the performance of the Book. Certain figures are brought to the precipice of signifying doubly. For example, the term *vol*, which often appears in the mathematical and logistical calculations as an abbreviation for "volume" also means "theft," a motif that is important for *The Book*.

Toward the beginning of the manuscripts, there are drafts of letters to Charles Morice and Edmond Lepelletier, as well as the draft of an unpublished article for the *National Observer*. The other types of text that appear in *The Book* are heterogeneous—they include poetry; symbolic and mathematical diagrams; plans for the material production of the text and its performance which take discursive, poetic, and logistical forms; graphic diagrams; and a kind of confessional mode in which such phrases are written as the following: "I am me — faithful to the / book."[40]

The Book, true to its concept, has no discernible beginning or end. Its movement is not linear, but differential and transversal. A reading method that is open to experimentation is thus called for. As much as the text performs its own poetic operation, it is in the reader's hands to decide what form this operation will take in the instant of reading.

---

[40] Mallarmé, *The Book*, 42.

THE BOOK

finish
consciousness

_____

And pains
too much
street

notorious
crime

double
place
crowd — my
square   /   *a — crime — sewer*

____ /

2[1]

of a
I revere Poe's opinion, no vestige ~~of~~ philosophy,
ethics or metaphysics will become transparent, ~~in the~~
~~poem; but if the necessity arises, as latent and included~~
I add that it is necessary, included ~~and~~ or latent.
~~both latent~~
~~and included.~~ [The song springs from an innate source, anterior
reflecting outside
~~illuminates everyone in one's self~~
to a concept, so purely that ~~reflecting without its knowledge~~
the thousand   some reality
~~all the~~ rhythms of images] To avoid ~~the gratuity of a~~ of
the   this
~~some~~ scaffolding remaining around ~~an~~ architecture,
does not imply there
spontaneous and magical! ~~only that doesn't mean~~
the lack   of   and subtle
~~that subtle~~ and powerful calculations ~~don't exist there~~
ignore them,   become
but we ~~refuse them or~~ they themselves ~~take place~~
unnoticed   ~~So~~   W
~~within us, repressed, mute.~~ Only ~~what~~
mysterious ~~mysterious summaries~~ on purpose.
genius ~~it requires~~ to be a poet; what ~~intuitive~~
~~of instict~~   simply   virginal,
lightning to contain, ~~which is only~~ life, ~~total, latent,~~
native
~~far off~~   ~~evoking~~
~~always reflecting everything~~
in its synthesis, ~~not illuminating thus always~~
and far illuminating everything
intellectual   of the
~~one of its aspects.~~ The   framework ~~of a concept~~

---

[1] Draft of a letter to Charles Morice, October 27, 1892.

poem, ~~held~~ in space which isolates the stanzas and
 conceals itself ~~and~~ takes place
amid the white of the paper; significative silence that it
   beautiful
is no less ~~difficult~~ to compose, than the
   ~~meritorious~~
   ~~glorious~~
verses.

       I often remain there,
       the same, my good Morice

3 (A)[2]

All my thanks, my dear fellow, for taking
care of this little book, ~~as and for~~ and for
       your   that you said
~~expressing the charming~~ word on Mass in Music,
       this   so true
or
~~and~~ of Requiem, ~~that~~ makes all I wished for
          that   ~~on~~
           music all
pure.

---

[2] Draft of a letter to Edmond Lepelletier, November 1, 1892.

$480 = 96 \times 5$ 24 times 240

$= \quad \begin{array}{c|c} 96 & 96 \\ \hline 96 & 96 \end{array}$ —x 384 x 5

480 480 = 960   1920 | x 3 = 5760
480 480 = 960   (+ 240   1/25th
                        = 6,000

12 x 480 |

————— - ——-
————— - ——-   384 x 5
                                      x 3

                                    384 x 15

————— - ——-
————— - ——-   384 to 24 cp. x 5
                                  = 384 to 120
                                        x 3

24 x 15 _____

                                  = to 360

4 (A)

or that th. is this that

<u>caused by |</u>
The Drama is   the Myst. of what follows — the Identity
                                                        (Idea) Self —
of the Theater and of the Hero through the Hymn
nature and man life
city

city and life   operation
= homeland   — the Hero
                                                <u>emanates</u> — the (maternal) Hymn
                                     that creates him, and ~~to his~~

        figure
                                     returns himself to the Th that he was —
                                                        this hymn ~~is hidden~~
                                     of the Mystery where ~~it is was~~ buried

        (

        but to which
        state does it appear
        badly at the beginning?   measure
                                                   Dr. while

            is only unsolvable because unapproachable
x   Dr ~~is not onl~~ (yes! whoever in the Universe has it
        ~~if one has~~ the idea of it, only at the state of glimmer,
    one does not have
    for it is resolved straight away, time enough to show its
        defeat, which unfolds dazzlingly —

the ~~lack~~   Drama is in the mystery
of the following equation   made of a double
                                                                     identity
                                                   equation or idea
that Th   if this is that
       is   that is this

the development of the hero   or hero
                                                   wrongly split in two
the summary of the th
As ~~Myst~~   is hymn
       Idea

                        idea
thus   Th = ~~mystery~~

and we
 draw from it   hero =   hymn
to redeem
this scission   and that forms a whole
                                       Dr or Mystery
                                       returning one into the other
                                       also

6 (A)

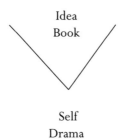

Idea
Book

Self
Drama

Th	Myst
The world	The year
Hero	Hymn
Man	Life

glory

genius   passion

~~health~~

~~life~~

(7-11)[3]

_____
N O
_____

Literature

Doctrine

7

~~The Enchanter of Letters, with a precision~~

7 (A)

III.

I list<u>en.</u> | ... To Life.. ~~especially social life,~~
~~to the popular and worldly gesture~~, to

                              — ~~Quotidian — isn't~~
              ~~say~~   ~~impose it on me!~~
~~it?~~   — ~~Such that you do it, suffer it, portray it~~
                              it

Jokers and criminals, novelists: you secularized priests, predictable that this charac-
ter   that would not efface any
cauterization, the daily ~~shower~~

---

[3] Pages 7–11 comprise the draft of an unpublished article written for the *National Observer* in January 1893.

III.

Banality! ~~and boredom~~

shower of banality that befalls you

     it   ~~I think you're odious~~

operates its washing without fail: ~~how I~~

                  ~~prolongation of~~ heralds of

~~hate you~~   and it's you   ~~writers~~   this error

~~curse you~~ ~~otherwise, you~~, the mass and

               universal

     ~~writers otherwise~~ than

the majority,＼   ~~than the~~ poor ~~sorcerers~~

     brothers, otherwise than   Kabbalists

     O ~~powerful~~

     ~~brothers~~

~~yesterday~~ soon

scorned by an artful anectode:~~, boredom~~:

             on the

            ~~on a~~ gust of wind if it's on your

    and I congratulate myself ~~if it's on your~~ side that ~~it~~

and ~~over~~ toward ~~you, the~~

        a gust of wind

——— ~~in~~ the last place it

breaks my shrug.   ~~You~~

        No,

   you   from

~~others~~ do not settle for ~~detaching~~

       and misunderstanding

    like them, ~~you others~~

      by ~~inattention~~

9 (A)

III.

<u>by inattention</u>
            operations   of it
to an ~~A~~art of ~~practices~~ which ~~is~~ are integral ~~part~~
                                      integral
                           and fundamental

   employ and perform
   ~~cultivate~~
to ~~honor~~ them, wrongly, isolated,
     it's another veneration
~~there still remains a piety~~, clum-
   ~~You~~   You ~~All~~   ~~all~~
sy. ~~But you~~ efface them right down
     initial   meaning
to the ~~original~~ sacred ~~sign~~.
     by ~~the presence~~ with
  Yes! ~~by the fact of~~ its twenty-four
signs   ~~to~~   exact-
~~letters~~, this Literature ~~or proper~~
ly named Letters, in this way

III.

multiple ~~quality~~
~~the~~ of   fusions
by ~~this innumerable~~   ~~multiple~~
as ~~its mysterious development~~ in
the figure   ~~and~~ then the
~~the phrases of rhythms~~ of phrases, the
verse, ~~entire~~ system organized ~~by~~ like
spiritual
a ~~mysterious~~ zodiac, implies ~~some~~
its own   ~~impersonal~~
~~a own proper~~ doctrine, ~~and, precise~~
some ~~impersonal~~   abstract, esoteric,
like ~~a mys~~ theology: based
notions
singly   ~~ideas~~
on the fact, ~~very simply,~~ that the ~~things~~
are such, or at a ~~point~~ of rarefaction
degree

11 (A)
14

III.

    the ordinary ~~common~~
beyond ~~any~~   ~~vulgar~~ achievement,
     cannot be expressed
that ~~they could not be spoken~~
     if not   ~~by the design~~   august
~~otherwise than~~ in ~~the molds or~~
     than with means,
typical and supreme,
       is
~~and~~ whose number, not more than their
       to them
own, ~~is not~~ unlimited.

summit   cathedr. circus
flowers   sea

dance-mime
                          |
block   face
ruin   bread   the dress
storm
forest |

                          |

relation
with
the hat

dividing into 4

---

[4] This isolated page is included in the transcription of the *Notes en vue du "Livre"* published in the Pléiade edition of Mallarmé's complete works in 1998, Stéphane Mallarmé, *Oeuvres complètes I*, ed. Bertrand Marchal (Paris: Gallimard, "Bibliothèque de la Pléiade" collection, 1998),1060. It is noted, in the *Notes et variants* of that volume, that this page is undoubtedly part of *Le Livre* although its precise placement is unclear (see page 1449).

12 (A)

Always this word of a human
language and which designates someone

 if it were spoken

halfway
 not seem to say the one he

to him
 called, ~~and while liste~~ lending an ear

head tilted
 a bit high* face smiling
to one side, ~~and bringing back~~ as who
 listening in order to obey, what follows
will obey — ~~and start again mind~~

~~far off, lik~~

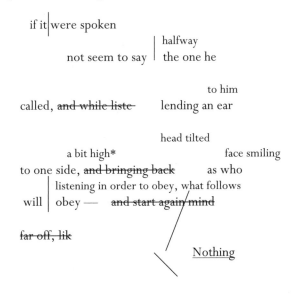

Nothing

all while we do the opposite

---

* for the word seemed to fall into depths
come from higher up than he

dark
 where he is

13 (A)

to mother

in the manner of a child ⌐~~showing~~contradicting *

~~espi~~ mischevious and

that head (scission, stage,) and ~~following the~~
~~one the body follows~~ that the body follows from the
opposite side to the possible source of
sound.

> ⌐ *as one who flees also*
>
> *fearful*

that he has been called thus trapped inside

the circle of a word ⌐ *here nothing said of*

the soul

mimicking

does he have herds

and his mystery

---

* yet he is so serious <u>this man</u> — has
all the stature of a man —

| but then vast —

serious kneels

14 (A)

Thus the word is not spoken for him
at this moment when he hears it, if it
ever was (no — he seems to say to
his
this doubt, recognized ~~the~~ free mind — he
not to the order, which, neutral, calls him and leaves him free — + ~~this word~~
was not) ~~and he will start again)~~
spoken, this word that is him there and retains, and all while
remaining.

he is pleased | the attitude which is that of a departure —
as to |
show it | tilted ahead, a foot ahead
to start again |

⌜ and reflects summit, mountain — by attitude —
diagonal ⌟
but

+
minus his friends, no chains.
does he tremble

without however leaving with the other foot — without
parting, yielding to the hidden order in the
firm and benevolent neutrality of this word
　　　exaggerates perhaps the secret challenge of his
act begun anyway
　　　　　~~or maybe it's to~~　　~~enter~~
　　　　　　　~~(crawl)~~

　　　　　　　　　　~~and shadow, block~~

　　~~of the~~
~~in challenge and pity~~

　　　　　　　　　　　　challenge
　　　　　　　　　that someone — this
　　　　　will not be him

　　　　　　　　　once summoned
　　　　　by this word and knowing who
　　　　　he is.
　　　　　　　　　　(power
　　　　　　　　　　　　of a word well said
　　　　　or maybe
　　　　　　　　　it's to

16 (A)

It's always you I
see on the shore

                                              as to recommence
this time with glory and bitterness to the past   the open air
        ~~despair~~

↓ when I left…

                                           [or broken
     (they disappear halfway but not without having thrown
                      ↑   women   reproachful tone (mine
                                                   (the +

                a beautiful homeland…
                     divine land
               more than a fiancée

     with deception and glory again
↑   to conquer

                     ↑ my only fiancée |_   the earth |_

                             or fiancée
                    and this returning dream

---

and interruption to fool the audience on the two!

~~the representatives of contemporary~~
~~humanity~~

but without the audience ~~know-~~
                    the crowd
~~ing the mystery~~ *here present*
in the room ~~while kno it they~~ *kn-*
ow the mystery

        ~~while hoping~~
        ~~A great event, audacious theft~~
~~of their prejudice~~
~~has been made~~

17 (A)

and as there was at the beginning,
in what he would repeat,
extending his arms, on the shore — and
that he thinks they are free — they are illumined,
free here

and from both sides
and since returning from both sides, by
                              here and there
a clever interlacing mixture of those
that one has seen from one side then from the other, the
double troupe, is there this

---

appearing there then as half
                    two halves of a troupe

times extending indeed their arms here
and there, as on two
shores very ~~distinct~~ far apart, ~~and~~
    between which,
but ~~from which~~ through the mind without
a doubt [through it] ~~those~~
~~who before were are there extend~~
       and ideal
a mysterious rapproche-
ment takes place, ~~that which sound~~ each of them
extending from where she is, ~~since she~~
has gone or
the arms to her absence

---

       hemisphere
    — and eye of the monster
     who watches them —

   but they're missing
     something

---

and reverie   arms crossed over absent
              breasts

19 (A)

from the other side, at once future
and past | one arm low, an-
                                                  other lifted, attitude of
                                                       the dancer

~~Such is that which~~
            Such is that which takes visible place
~~in s~~ he, omitted

~~But since it's for them alone that he was~~   for this
And he hears the girls' laughs — you will bring me —   dream
this, that — diamond — diamond — and he he-   is made
ard only that (he, glory, they lie down, fortune, etc.)   of their
they stopping their laugh in the diamond bird   purity
truly appeared — there and that they would all like to have   kept
                                                         all to
                                                         them

open on middle 2nd ~~ground~~ | solitary

~~party~~   in itself — ~~party~~ that extends

to the mysterious before, like the

ground —   — preparation for the party

=   interlude

confusion of the two

or = *

with interruption of the open ground   scission in

the ground

— starting again where

we leave it

=   interlude

before only   (recall of the party (regrets, etc.)

(and growing

from the middle.

and   the curtain lifts — falll — | room

and ground

Corresponding to ground   the beyond

and mysterious before — corresponds to

what hides the ground (canvas, etc.) makes its

mystery —

---

ground = room   * to lustres

21 (A)

the electric arabesque
lights up behind — and the two
veils

— sort of sacred tearing of the
veil, orchestra — or tears —

and two beings at once bird
and perfume — similar to the two from on
pulpit
high (balcony) lik

---

the egg   church

                                        the keys of the boundless
            Sad and magnificent vision
            What is ~~this tr   or the~~
            The remains of a large palace,
    — large as a city — or
of a ~~large~~ city unchanging as a
lone palace.

            This is all the echo says —
double and lying, interrogated
by the voy~~aging spirit~~ (wind)

            All we know is that she

_____

at least that some ship, floating city   triangular
has returned — more city of the future poet   rocking

23 (A)

lies in the tenebrous past —
indeed the desert took her back —
unless she lies in
the future — ~~impossible~~ closed to
~~for suddenly~~ human eyes, there
~~forgetting and~~   ~~at the ground~~

In front of — double fountain, where its
    dream
cursed people — who sleeps — , no
longer comes reflecting itself *

in the look of its immense pride

Which could — be the remains in
the past — and what strange adventure
precipitated thus this race.

Modern is this calm — tamer-man
~~function of pre~~
— tell us ~~your~~ the secret

— During that time — dioramic
curtain deepened — shadow
stronger and stronger, as if hollowed out
by it — by the mystery —

The blind ~~lowere~~ undid itself — with —
the assets that couldn't return the
music and which are there, elephants, etc.

25 (A)

The wild beasts have been seen
indeed on the ground of the blind, in ~~this~~
~~im~~ this pause [and have never dare enter
                    fire
there — as if terrified — they have
as if glimpsed one who is like them,
but invisible, and have leapt —
two times — ~~first a panther~~
~~against~~ as one against the other
— the snakes who whisper
hate to them, leapt through the rings
                              mobiles of the
of the snake, to show that no
mirror there | then returned suddenly

                    | the ignorant beasts
but in the middle

pacified . and carrying on their backs
~~the wom~~ these two ideal
women, ~~pl~~ passed there. (~~they do~~
          attracted by
they don't dare go farther be-
cause great fire in the middle, so deserted
voyager — tempts night — from the tent to the
palace — (or vessel)

> hunt the two beasts
> the most untamable
> white bear
> black panther
> elephant held by the
> two

beasts on two feet, expressing desire to
see!   [while we arrange —

27 (A)

and it will come about — that torture ~~of~~
ignored — ~~mak~~ modesty — hunger and love
of skies

—————— the old man —
under the crowd influence—that he
~~holds it~~ is

— will appear — to have
suffered the present tortures —
guillotine

gunfire
while dying of
hunger
or else

doubt, all is there
has only one louis!
hesitates (to dine)
both   or
in Th?,   drinks

hunger of your flesh thirst of your eyes
final

to go — "into the trick of death from
hunger" ~~jus~~ if — etc. | crowd | torture ignored
here

until the grave inclu-
sively

she is — and not
she is fictively, condi-
tional (literarily)
he does this to show

what would happen if...

but she must
according to him, for
cover herself | dying of hunger gives him the right
to start over — other star, summit —
skies...

— after nonetheless
victim of his trick

29 (A)

```
                          fallen skies
           is it the wind, that closed the

           door [old tale — castle]

                    the priest?
```

```
              —— sort of confinement
                     1 / 2
           and to delight in his accumulated
           power there — for it's in the idea
                          (unjust
           of condemnation  to death that he
           accumulates it — skies —

                          free thought in itself.

                i.e. to make oneself

                like a priest deprived of everything
```

priest must ignore, for human glory, the mystery of
woman — thus (child in his legs) everything will resolve itself
                                        by that —

            but the trick [thus: of we two, etc.]
     is yet not found the searched-out mystery (if not assisted, crowd?)
     and it's only there in the grave that he can find it
     thus —
           on the other hand it's necessary that young
         in him indulging himself in the dream of setting in motion the great
                              machine, a worker

     man   — ~~come~~ but who
     is only old — ~~com~~ come
     into the grave (burying fiancée there
priest — confinement   \
     unknown)   \ so as to know
     mystery, before getting married
     — what to say to children

           ———————— source — old man
         fight — and there the whole played out

             worker left
                old man escaped —

—————————————————————————

you're already thinking of that? of them
       It's strange
             — leave this care to ancestor?   love, you.

31 (A)

—— that young man should come sacred
as a death — the mystery of love —
— he this other need

⌐ let us unify our two needs

———————————————

and the old man leaves
existing — for it is old age —
Fictive death —
as youth is fictive
birth.

he leaves ideally — not in reality
and friendless and parentless, not by the thought of others
but by his own — he thinks — or of crowd *
—- the door has closed around it — for
the resilience is on the other hand — that he doesn't have
the right, etc. to these skies —
    we have /   the mystery —
that if   / found, but he's cloistered himself
        for death is necessary to
there to find,   know the mystery

        ⌐such is the trick⌐
            tower

  this must be so
         worker
 until clothed child
    what he must have been by being born but has made himself so
of these skies — appeared — comes
to deliver in him — instead of the
priest the old man — who
will be haunted

---

* so that if inferior if not by his own, superior
for he crowds us, etc. ashes — so total —

33 (A)

until child he had inside him
(worker) ~~who~~ instead of priest — who
suffers unduly from this confinement —
                    from
is hungry and thirsty (rage) complains in the name
of justice, of being cloistered this way in the
priest — priest (chaste and dying of hunger) chaste
child in him — dying of hunger, old man.

            returns to draw from it.....
from mystery that we can't know
except by performing it — love —
proof — child

Read

12 persons.

Read. the

mass — the com | nion

each one having only
the volume I grant myself

— but supposed
paying 2 f. per pers —
effaced.
at the price of theft, hear
for nothing —

_____

voice. phonogr.

35 (B)

I am me — faithful to the book,

———

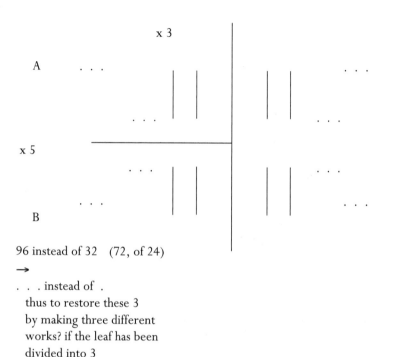

x 3

A

x 5

B

96 instead of 32   (72, of 24)

→

. . . instead of .
  thus to restore these 3
  by making three different
  works? if the leaf has been
  divided into 3

          multiply by five

↓   ~~two pl~~

              Operat.
A │   Read.
  │ the same wrk. presents itself
B │ differently twice.
          reduce it to the same?

37 (A) (2)

. . .

    . . .

= 6
= 12 half-f.
for 12 persons   or 6 double seats   the
                                          2 sessions

and   . . .

  . . .

  same thing   only ever half   same day
= for 24 pers.   the gap for double $\neq$
                    the paper

(2 cps.)

    me 25th.

these 5 f. why?   5 francs?   25th place.

---

5 real fr — if I assume them —
    to come see a work whose price is —
                unity...

half

≠   10 doubles or 20 ~~of~~ singles

and then so that ~~20~~ per year   start again

———————————

| | | | | |

another book corresponding to that one —
on the 6

                    — which would make 3 years

                                        3 times

          — each year
                    120 leaves   (1000 f. per leaf)

                    360 persons
                              Year —

~~12 pers~~

39 (A) (1)

importance — value (thus gilded edges)

if

paper — a book, proportions of 5 by 6?

3

times in height its thickness laid flat

and its width 4 times   the relation is in

base

the thickness

the height indicates the number of lines   18

the width — their fragmented length   12

the thickness the reach of their addition — if from 1 to 2/3

or if the height is reduced

to 12. everything happens between the width and the thickness

and the defalcation of the number of lines gilded edges at the top

indicates the number of volumes

in which one is resolved

thus 5 (Or 6?) ~~books~~ volumes   laid flat   superimposed

= the height of one upright — and a whole of volumes

upright = ~~the height of~~ the block produced by ~~one~~ the

same number of vols. laid flat.   the block

~~identical~~

— ~~double the block laid flat or upright~~

≠ a book can
thus only contain
a certain quantity
of matter — its
value —
ideal
without numbers that is

that it should be   maybe there are only
more or less   not high or low enough — without val.
that what is — to sell it   thus infinite
is too expensive and not enough.   — ideal — but value
(pure — diamond)

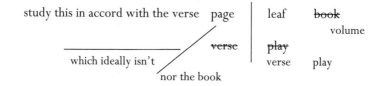

study this in accord with the verse   page   │   leaf   ~~book~~
                                                │   volume
    _____ ╱ ~~verse~~   │   ~~play~~
        which ideally isn't   ╱   │   verse   play
                          ╱ nor the book

40 (A) (2)

this block can thus in no way form a square
but on the façade, seeing the backs, for example, either upright
or laid flat — but it would not have it in depth or

it occupies
a rectangle   *— it would be necessary to triple, this block, upright*
trunk—   *or laid flat, to triple it in the direction of the width*
laws of this   *to form*
rectangle

                    in that, when seen straight on, will be-
of
proportions   come ~~the~~ thickness   (relation of ~~the size~~
                                                                    thickness
                                                          by two times
                             of the book and of its width laid flat or upright thus signa-
                                             ling it in gold — it stays the same

it has not fallen   ~~its width, when in a block, becomes its~~
by chance,   ~~thickness~~   streak of gold, to trace it in
        consecration   thickness and width
of a singe one —   given as exactly
we get out of it —   as tightly as possible.
open it
onto
thickness

                    its width when, in a block
                    becomes its thickness — and if one found it
                    a disproportion in the block, upright or
                                             laid flat,
                                        which is equivalent

separations   which would only be
of the book
which opens   in this lack of width
disjunctions   (depth
of the relations   born ~~no~~, as
of its different   thickness, not
measures   the width —

        then, all while giving up on the
~~impersonal~~ square
      whatever the most that one could do

41 (A) (3)

or to divide   6 v or 12

would be to double, for example this thickness —
edges to edges. and one would obtain the
      in some direction, laid flat or upright
two blocks a <u>rectangle</u> presenting its
height as well as its width or 2 widths of vol.
     or thickness   each vol
        here—   becoming the
                                        1st 6 x 6
   a new side of   36
   its surface ~~equals~~
   such as 24 : 18 (width or thickness)
    or 4 : 3
      ~~and as for~~

   it will be necessary for these six other vols. to be
  the same ones — but presented differently —   (⌊   ⌋ ?)
  to establish an identity   or
                                                   ⌟ ⌊

          the Wrk. in 6 v. having
          given itself twice.

     The Readings having no other goal   fix a price
                                    in
than to show these scientific relations —   discovery of the book
                                   in its value

etc.   but by the same token identifying myself with the author
                  constituting an audacious act of courage for myself

of the one — who cannot seize the book

or its value.   ⌐ shown that self, if fallen
from the sky and answering to all

                                   — who can hold to it

qualified — etc.,

              as to oneself — 1ˢᵗ

                    without revealing its author to oneself

          no — the one who wrote that
                No one — genius alone

       or if not the author the 1ˢᵗ reader
it's by whoever reads it — and last if he
seizes it —   honor is to
                            edit it

       ⌐ to find in what precedes
       ∟ the relations with 5 and 3 — Read

43 (A) (5)

and for this reader the book is pure block —
transparent — he reads inside, makes it out — knows
                              showing
in advance — ~~tone~~ where it is — what must be —
          or finish   ~~silent~~
                                        junctions — relations ⌟

Folds

—| -   far here. 20 vol

series —
folds on each side

                and because of that
come back, to the split   addition of a
                    leaf in the opposite direction
                      against
                            death
                            rebirth?
                  for xxxxxxx

one never
turns a fold in the opposite
direction   — there is another leaf
             to respond to the possibility
             of this other direction.

                                          series of folds
                              gilding —
                                       on hard
the fold which on one   cardstock (as
side alone —   formerly in bookbinding)
arrests the gaze —
and masks.

45 (A)

= 96
48 − 48

96

x

5   x 5 | 4 x   x 3 = 144 − 144
                                    (288)
                              x 5

1440 p

= 45 leaves
x 2
90 x | 4 = 360

240 + 240 = 480

xxx

180   180 = 360

5760 p

240

25th

46 (B)

The 4 of each
year

One of the 4 books
having 5 different
motifs —
┌ distributed
95 x 5
=

47 (B)

It is necessary, at a
glance by the succession
of sentences —
With place = leaf
— etc.

that everything appear
in this Program

Remains 1 vol of
320   (20 leaves)
160 leaflets
cut in 3
= the 480 invitation
cards —
with indication of nothing_____
                                    draft
        on 20 of 384
        x 3

49 (B)

or 3 v. of 320
if the leaf is
not cut

5 years. The lustre

51 (B)

sitting where they like
in their places
3 changeable
the question is knowing   leaves
dignitaries
if the 24 come
at the same time and a
single reading

————————

———— or if
or else if 3
readings say at 8
x 3
or at 8 (with 2 assistants)

the manuscript alone
is mobile —

that would multiply
by 3

$$
\begin{array}{r}
240,000 \\
3 \\
\hline
720,000
\end{array}
$$

$24 \qquad 25^{th}$

$\underline{\times 4} \qquad \quad 4$

$96 \qquad = 100$

$\underline{\times 500}$

$\underline{48000}$

4 *printed at 3*

of 3 vol

printed at 4000

53 (B)

is it too much with 3 —
immobilized
and 1 l.
or
vol with 3 mobile l.?

3
mobile volumes

4
copies

4 ———
———
———
———

x *5 years*

the lustre

if volume triples
to 3 f — whose use
has been shown
to link them

1 f for expenses

xxxxxx

material —
2 f. remain for
me —

the 2 make a 3rd
copy

55 (B)

the book   eliminates
time   ashes

toward the relation in \
       of non coexistence

———————————

toward the relation
of 8 printed pages

———————

the paper is only white if
    the leaf is virginal
        nothing
            in mind

57 (B)

The hero
changes Dr. into
mystery — returns
dr. to mystery
            — plays itself out —
of which it has the Idea —

and this latter which is in
                    example
                            vol.
the state of <u>Th.</u> — he
returns it into Hymn

58 (B)

(1

Read

I thus make myself

for the pleasure of

showing myself.   under a

pretext that —

the book

letter.

~~to the world~~

⌐for

I could make use

of the book precisely to

progagate it — I don't want,

stop myself there

— appear   be it!

5

necessary to

plunge back into it and

repeat

59 (B) (2)

I̶ ̶m̶a̶k̶e̶   to show myself
                                          the one —
                                                    who knows

                        in the Idea
of all. s. ent.
                  for one must suppose
         that of me —   under this
           guise of study — that
                                  their action
                                        entices
                                                alone —

    +

                                        to identify myself
                  with the book —

these remarks
              that in
air
                  eternal
performance
dr — and symphony
— an actor —
              I
wondered earlier
muslin spring
hopes of a single
sun   (against proofs
       just a cold — forced
to be interested in it

a generosity in invi-
ting… people —
tickets, etc.. who
would like so mu<u>ch</u> —
to be aware

to find me
the only one
to come —   —

if not all that —
truly they have
nothing sacred. The
proof the war.
          muder —
erected.
          — the only
happy crime

61 (B) (4)

perhaps
          — and to efface that—
for I'm supposed to come
one of them —

       on what to fix
the sum of invita-
tion
  — always
am I bound —

so mediocre, to
kill another
      — erected
in — glory

it's like a borrowed thing
above —   if this made
in the world's favor
— to be returned to the
people — in copies
cheaply

> with
> my humble gain —

The convent — we
all become it —
          make
same thing —

          with

— it lacks
agency.

63 (B) (6)

and to replace bookstores
with beggars   O
                              concierge!)
— the Sum —
equal to that —

Consecration
          divine presence
the actor before
to remain invisible
          he is there
_____

480
500
240,000

Read.
        all is there

because it is not
over
— *it cannot be*
— *the cities were*
— *the* —
        all that futile
collapsed —
        because

64 (B) (1)

made
no printing lower   The Text is printed at 400
    10 and 4   quadruple is printed at 10
If printed at 400   supposed   and 1 or 4 works
    If kept for me   = 400 v.

I grant them to myself
by my readings.
the 10 copies or 40 v.
360 vol. or
90 cps. remain

— the 10 copies —
are each a variant of the 10 Readings.

each session

and me   being quadruple

9 persons present x 4

to the readers.   = 36.

10 quadruple sessions

numbering ~~40 sessions and~~ 360 places

for the 40 volumes

and 360 leaves

1 volume per session.

9 leaves per 9 places.

each vol. has 9 leaves
each session has 9 places

66 (B)

|

my newspaper

to be able to print   360
                to a thousand
              instead of charging
            ~~36~~ a thousand fr.
              to 360 persons
                         per vol

charging 100 f. for each vol.
which is not — in advance —

I take 100 f. For ex 4 f. such the 5 of three

288   24
48   12

+ 12 me
summarizing

68 (B)

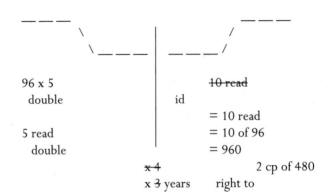

96 x 5
  double

5 read
  double

id

~~10 read~~

= 10 read
= 10 of 96
= 960

x~~4~~

x ~~3~~ years

2 cp of 480

right to

— — —

—

—

1 1/2 leaves
of the 5 id

1 leaf

play and leaf

that times 2
= 20 leaves
leaves = 320
x   3
=   960

240 + 240
= 480

= 6 Read

times 3

= 24

start over

4 times (of 320)

24
pers.
sessions
me
of 320

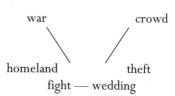

war   crowd

homeland   theft

fight — wedding

70 (B)

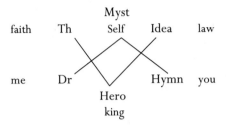

play each
day —

360
——

20 l⁄

7200

800
—— 80
————

72 (B)

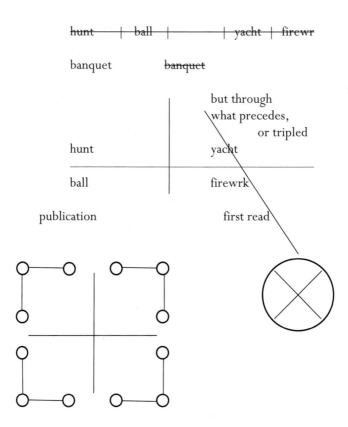

~~hunt~~ | ~~ball~~ | | ~~yacht~~ | ~~firewr~~

banquet   ~~banquet~~

but through
what precedes,
or tripled

hunt   yacht

ball   firewrk

publication   first read

hunt

burial   baptism

banquet   yacht

ball   firewr.

 hunt
   war   theft
    (wedding)
 firewr

73 (B)

$$1, 10 \ldots \ldots \qquad\qquad 4$$

$$—\ \ —\ \ — \qquad\qquad\quad 36$$

$$9$$

74 (B)

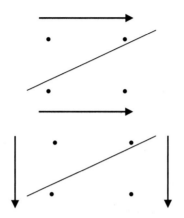

75 (B)

                                        Read.
                     the printing decreases
                            — until
                                    and the paper
                     comes and takes the place
                     —   until a price
                     fusion of the two
                                    minimum —

                     to stop —

                       until that very moment
                       to print on beautiful paper
                       or edit separately —
                                    to search —

— and the organ
~~re~~   literature
becomes so quickly exte-
rior, loses
quickly — the notion
— of mystery —
— that the organ —

76 (B)

and conversely
begun again in ⌐ ∟

A B C		second
C A B		in 3
B C A		begun again
		and
A C B		half
C B A		the leaf
B A C		takes off
		on the double

but as ⌐ and ∟   is worth 5

= 90

x 4 (5 x 4 = 20) 360

77 (B)

Read

read outside

and that the book
presents itself
like this

and

• V   V •   • V   V •

necessity of folding

78 (B)

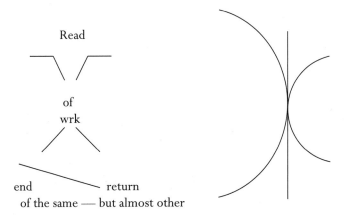

Read

of
wrk

end
of the same — but almost other — return

each of the six concurrents
      3 for one wrk — 3
    withdraws for the other
    with its price of a <u>thousand</u> or 4
    francs and it's <u>the same</u>
        thus 6000 f

    who alone had the idea
        of — of — these games
      these —

80 (B)

Hunt   tablecloth   yacht

banquet   gun   — — —

                                      firewrk
              — — —   theft __ __ __

              ball. mirage.
                        thus challenge, gun)

Read   480 + 480

240   x 3 = 320

2 per page
converted into the
leaf —

yacht

hunt   goal   motif
        line

bounds   firewrk

number of readers
edition — firewrk

82 (B)

2 read. per year
each inviting
the other.

———————

week

———————

240 p   from the page
to the leaf

at 240 f.

an appearance

S. of Reading
Sessions of the Dr
and of the Hymn.
                    Th
    is
    —— by the hero

the development of the Dr
in Th   the hymn   ⌈but
it was necessary that the hymn
be in the state of th

84 (B)

reat by Dr.
in case
someone should take credit for it

Th
play
verse book

———

Read. Sessions
of the Dr and the Hymn
— or of Myst. and Ideas

identical in the

Th. ⌐ or <u>Idea</u>

operated   eliminated)

86 (B) (3)

It's enough to satis-
fy
our mind —

of the equivalence
of light con-
tained in a <u>lustre.</u>

The lustre ensures
the Th.
which is enough for the mind.

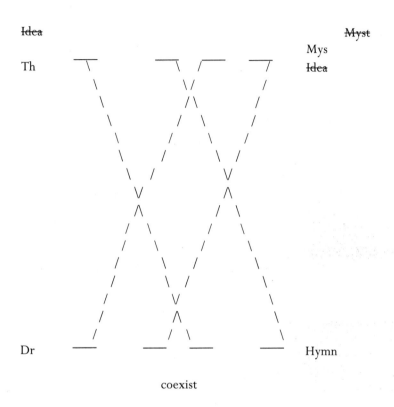

coexist

1/2 Dr 1—1/2 Myst 1; while 1/2 Myst 2..

88 (A)

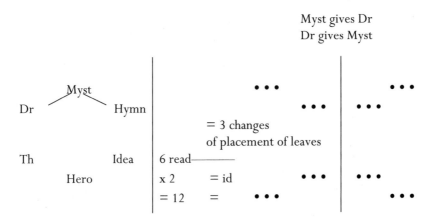

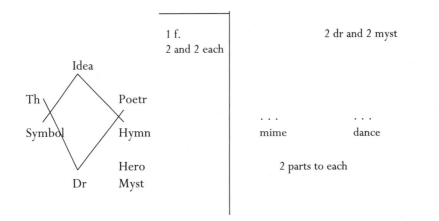

Each ~~The~~ text of the Wrk is given twice

———

~~only 4 halves coexist~~ are only the same thing all returned
                and
Myst ~~Is only~~ and Dr. ~~returned~~   and presenting
                , Dr. and myst.
the one outside what
the other hides inside.

Dr. the characters outside and Myst. inside
~~Myst~~

90 (A)

24 places, of foundation.

(in 8 of 3 = 24)

(whatever the number of real assistants,
if there was only the Reader

the operator

and the 25th is the operator
there are only 20 leaves :
consequently they are
not for the assistants
and the operator grants himself them.

. . . . . | . . . . .

. . . . . | . . . . .

volumes   one,   ~~each~~

These four ~~books~~ are ~~the two~~

each

two ~~halves, the~~ half of the one

each

compared with ~~the~~ half of the other

~~in two different directions~~, which

gives thus two sessions.

92 (A)

20 v. of 384 — in 4 parts, being 5 by 5
(384 x 5 = 1920) or 1 play.   2 = 3840 p. or
10 of 384. There are only 2 — which give once
2 plays in one direction, another time 2 plays in the other.
The same text twice.

being   384 x 5 | 384 x 5
      = (the 384 being as complete
              samples or 96 x 4)

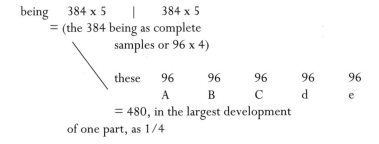

      these   96   96   96   96   96
                  A   B   C   d   e
      = 480, in the largest development
  of one part, as 1 / 4

480 supreme limit
of a burst *

To obtain in 3 times
the development **   480 — self-identical
or arranged in the opposite direction
960

by

~~160 95 x 5~~

160 x 3 — arranged as 1st x 3, 2nd x 3, etc. up to 10th
= 48 (x 10 = 480 x 2 = 960)
or 96 x 10.

each session or play
being a <u>game</u>, a fragmen-
tary perform-
ance, but this being
enough.
3 concurrent, reduplication

* firewrk
** sail, one appearance
of the book yacht.

94 (A)

A

Be it to win, by self-identity. play —
320 = 320   or qualified
            the right   to a truth)

16 x 10

x 2 x 2

to repeat ~~it~~ in the opposite direction
the volume

volume = play.

B

[thus 12 vol of 320 giving, xx while di-
viding itself, the text of 24

we ~~make~~ to make two copies of each
    have the right

here is the first motif of editing, book.

B

is it to begin
with the end?

[printer satisfied, one and another
the same]

this: 12 times (and in double 24 — the 24 persons always
present.
representing the entirety of the Wrk.
each a volume? or session, i.e. play

thus

320 × 3 = 960   480 + 480
    ×4
    ———
    3840

96

from

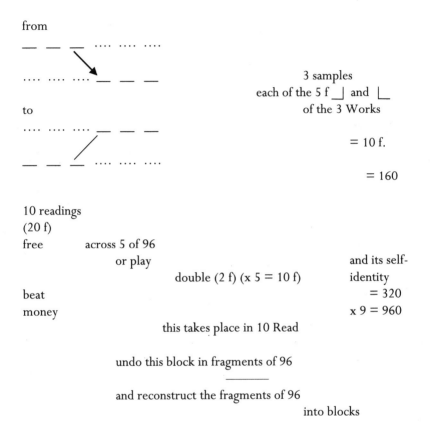

3 samples
each of the 5 f ⌐ and ⌐
of the 3 Works

to

= 10 f.

= 160

10 readings
(20 f)
free   across 5 of 96
                or play   and its self-
                          double (2 f) (x 5 = 10 f)   identity
beat   = 320
money   x 9 = 960

          this takes place in 10 Read

undo this block in fragments of 96
                        ————

and reconstruct the fragments of 96
                                into blocks

98 (A)

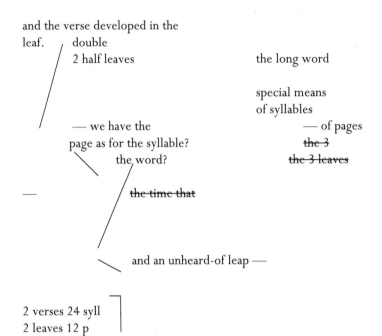

page. line verse —

          from page to verse

              and the book

and the verse developed in the
leaf.   double
        2 half leaves   the long word

                          special means
                          of syllables

      — we have the   — of pages
page as for the syllable?   ~~the 3~~
       the word?   ~~the 3 leaves~~

—   ~~the time that~~

         and an unheard-of leap —

2 verses 24 syll
2 leaves 12 p

                      each sound —
                  syllable is gold

The exterior pages unbound p in the middle
free — are the extremities, the farthest one
could go or a leaf.   it cannot
                    double

therefore be followed by another — it
can't if there are others t   6
          than to receive them in the interior —
correction — once all undone — and,
the gun. even — once one has played
on this that there could be nothing —

          the number of intercalations thus
          reinforcements
forming reduplications. i.e. following
the interior is only to —

                              $3 \times 2 = 6$
                    the 3 of the 3 leaves

          12×3
          $= 36 \times 10$
half printed
          thus to double   5

100 (A)

2 leaves
the title
on the verso
     of one — which becomes recto
          — on the recto of
              the other — which
        becomes verso.

     both
It shows in this way
     alone   — identity of the Book made out.

————————

all that there is extracted from the leaf — developing it —
    light what escapes from it — all that must
    be seen on this virgin white in the blink of an eye.
    without sign characters

    it is developed — it is stopped ~~unti~~ just before
the great ~~develop~~ interior opening, gun
or we will know if something or nothing

              other than all
                that is ,

        double
so that developed   cancel
it stays at the threshold
    to write its repercussions
        echo to the Pages

100 (A) b

Nonetheless ~~and~~ this event comes abou

101 (A)

.. ..

X

.. ..

.. ..

X

.. ..

producing both

play   newspaper
xx

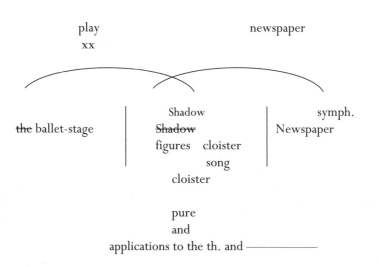

~~the~~ ballet-stage   Shadow   symph.
                    ~~Shadow~~   Newspaper
                    figures   cloister
                           song
                 cloister

pure
and
applications to the th. and ———————

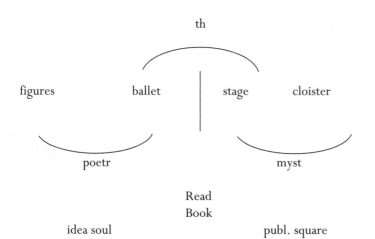

th

figures   ballet   stage   cloister

poetr   myst

Read
Book

idea soul   publ. square

103 (A)

			Theater	Mystery
Read.			~~Book~~	Verse
or			Figure	

Middle-term   Dr
hiding and showing   Book
pages] <u>Theater</u>, as Mystery   [cl.   hero   hymn
                                          man   song

by an operation called <u>Poetry</u> [1/2 cl   Poetry or Orch

   this in favor of the <u>Book</u>.

on one hand the motifs and songs │ the figures and cloister, on the other
            summits   │   (banquet)   ruin

opera   .   ballet   stage   .   cloister

      Th   Myst.
 xx. Poetr.

            The modernized whole. i.e. put under
        everyone's power, contemporarily applied,
             according to the Dance. (child)

Idea   Dr
(soul)   (publ. square)

th   Myst

one aspect

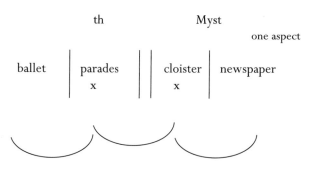

the other aspect

~~two forms of the same~~
~~equation~~
~~each term~~
~~occupying the centers~~

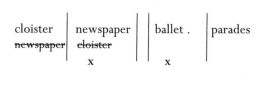

work single and triple
from 4 to 12
the same equation is given twice,
differently; and each term is now
be it 8

105 (A)

equation under a Janus god, total, proving itself

~~the two copies~~   ≠

motifs song	ballets — parades	figure Th
pure	movement	personal
summit etc.	adjoined with immobility	cloister and hero
song		

ballets	pure motifs figure	parades Myst
	songs. cloister	——————— impersonal
	myst. with coloration	and hymn

Reading
and modernities

≠ and for that
to take the halves
(480   30 leaves, the en-
tirety being of 960, 60
leaves)

= 4 x 2 (1/2) = 8
960 x 4 = 1920
        3840
or 480 x 8
or 1920 x 2

| or 160 x 12 |
| or 160 x 24 |
| + 160 1/25th |
| = 4000 |

of each of the

4 works

240 leaves
2 copies = 480 leaves.

480 leaves
+ 20 remaining
= 320 = 160 x 2
(1/25th)

a fragment or half represents
in pages what is on the leaf — is
from the page to the leaf.

106 (A)

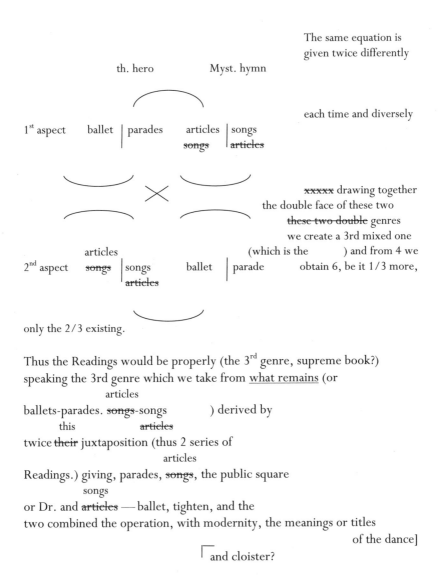

The same equation is
given twice differently

th. hero   Myst. hymn

each time and diversely

1st aspect   ballet | parades   articles | songs
                                    songs | articles

xxxxx drawing together
the double face of these two
these two double genres
we create a 3rd mixed one

articles   (which is the   ) and from 4 we
2nd aspect   songs | songs   ballet | parade   obtain 6, be it 1/3 more,
               articles

only the 2/3 existing.

Thus the Readings would be properly (the 3rd genre, supreme book?)
speaking the 3rd genre which we take from <u>what remains</u> (or
                    articles
ballets-parades. songs-songs   ) derived by
          this   articles
twice their juxtaposition (thus 2 series of
                              articles
Readings.) giving, parades, songs, the public square
          songs
or Dr. and articles — ballet, tighten, and the
two combined the operation, with modernity, the meanings or titles
                                                   of the dance]
                    ⌐ and cloister?

to obtain silence, and be sure that the dignitaries at least

At each Session   be 8

8 triple places (= 24 persons + me $1/25^{th}$ on the one hand as to the

persons, and $1/9^{th}$ as to the places: I who multiply myself, single and triple)

implies 24 leaves, or 3 leaves (triple place) x 8

Each session ~~takes place 5 times, and there are 8: or 40 v.~~

(as many as guests who, unwittingly, ~~xxx~~ represent the secret of the session.

and it's I who binding and summing up the whole, ~~form~~ amass these 24 leaves

as a combined whole = 384 p.

in a parallel way ~~two~~ per session, or day   two in one day, with different audience.

There are ~~two sessions of~~ Readings ~~and Interpretation~~ — and in each ~~the~~ a

in which

differently ~~interpreted~~ motifs or text: that establishes two currents, ~~which~~

| verse |

with one, two ~~different copies~~ of the Text, thus differentiated

different of the same wrk for these ones or those ones, according to preference —

ten | | interpretations

be it 48 (for 50) persons and 2 vol. of 384 p.

of the same double Reading

for there are 10 sessions in all = 480 for 500 persons)

per 500.

I take

108 (A)

2

10 to 10 equal by the text and different interpretation

~~10~~ books or one
thus 20 copies
double

⌐ reconstituted by my hand, and to be sold or edited as such —
each one to be printed at 500? 10,000. my right, to establish it —
each one will become the prototype of an
edition

~~and I leave 480 of them in circulation~~
which compose the whole ensemble
and I leave 480 of them in circulation
which, at 20 vol to form an
ensemble, make 24 copies
the 25th of which I have —

⌐ that can be executed 9 times for
9 works)

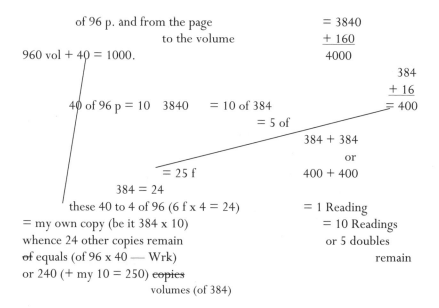

of 96 p. and from the page   = 3840

　　　　　　to the volume   + 160

960 vol + 40 = 1000.   4000

　　　　　　　　　　　　　　　　　　　　　　　384

　　　　　　　　　　　　　　　　　　　　　+ 16

40 of 96 p = 10　3840　　= 10 of 384　　= 400

　　　　　　　　　　　= 5 of

　　　　　　　　　　　　　　384 + 384

　　　　　　　　　　　　　　　or

　　　　　= 25 f　　　400 + 400

　　384 = 24

these 40 to 4 of 96 (6 f x 4 = 24)　　= 1 Reading

= my own copy (be it 384 x 10)　　　= 10 Readings

whence 24 other copies remain　　　or 5 doubles

of equals (of 96 x 40 — Wrk)　　　　　remain

or 240 (+ my 10 = 250) copies

　　　　volumes (of 384)

Be it also ~~Be it~~ 240 leaves per copy

　　　　　　　e volume which consists of 24 l

　　　or from the leaf, through the copy, ~~also~~

that times 4　　~~of the vol. which consists of 24 l~~ — to the copy (240

110 (A)

and Interpretation of the Wrk.   of the Text   unities
Readings of the Wrk.   3-3-9 —— 9-3-3
                                                          9   ——   9

of the Book   in the night
Sessions of Interpretation of the Wrk.   in costume

                                          readings per
Readings   guests   Sessions or   guests
10 ~~Sessions~~, each with 10 ~~persons~~, at 2 per day or 20 ~~persons per day~~
                         Reading   per session
one of which, at each ~~Session~~ reducing the audience to 9 (x 2 = 18), starts, me,
                                                     they unite their effort
knowing what it's about, to interpret (he has seen clearly, the electr. glimmer
has been his mind)

                                                            Sessions
                                                          = 5 ~~days~~
                                  —————   20 sessions per year,
(x 2 = 100 persons, or really 90. │ that times 4 be it ~~per year,~~ or in one
                                   │ year spread out over life. The 4 make
                                   │ (Book, same and void, insofar as
                                   │ central, angel)
                                                            ~~listeners~~
Each Reading is of one vol. or 10 leaves, = 160   360 ~~guests~~, and
and double = 320 (x 5 = 1600)   me the 40 others of 400, (Year
                                           number of the Book printing
                                           = 20 sessions
                                               combining two
                                               Readings.

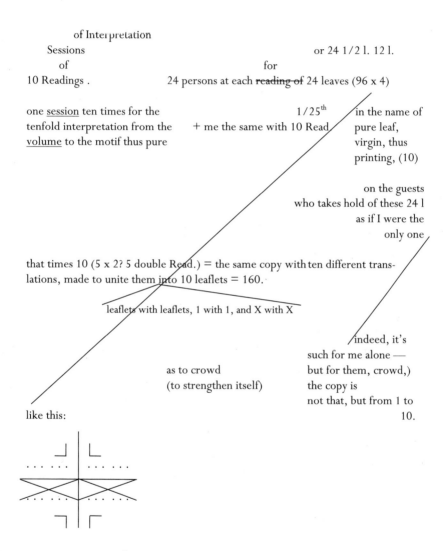

of Interpretation
Sessions   or 24 1/2 l. 12 l.
    of   for
10 Readings .   24 persons at each ~~reading of~~ 24 leaves (96 x 4)

one <u>session</u> ten times for the   1/25ᵗʰ   in the name of
tenfold interpretation from the   + me the same with 10 Read   pure leaf,
<u>volume</u> to the motif thus pure   virgin, thus
                                                                 printing, (10)

                                                        on the guests
                                                who takes hold of these 24 l
                                                        as if I were the
                                                            only one

that times 10 (5 x 2? 5 double Read.) = the same copy with ten different trans-
lations, made to unite them into 10 leaflets = 160.

        leaflets with leaflets, 1 with 1, and X with X

                                                    indeed, it's
                                                such for me alone —
                        as to crowd   but for them, crowd,)
                        (to strengthen itself)   the copy is
                                                not that, but from 1 to
like this: 10.

        or series of leaflets
A copy is thus given 10 times differently. Each copy

112 (A)

~~There are~~   4 Readings are given per year   over
~~The Sess~~   5 years
                                         = 60 sessions
                each of 3 sessions   20 Read
                                      = 60 volumes
                                    20 ~~copies~~
                                      texts

      The session, implies ~~a volume~~ the confrontation of a
fragment of book   or volume —
~~volume~~ with itself,   be it: the development of the leaf,
~~in 3, a~~ as to the text, in 3, in its quadruple aspect, (: :)
twice ~~= 8~~ (proving that <u>it is</u> that)

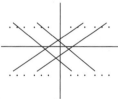

      it offers, uniformly, two times 4 places
occupied, for a dignitary, and two assistants, or the three, as needed: i.e.

(each one) ~~multiplied by 3 = 12~~ + 12 = 24   (= 384 p)
      Of each Reading three sessions is given and three volumes read, which makes
                              the same book

    A place relates to a leaf.   work
    A session to a volume.   text
                         ~~Book~~
    The Reading finally, has the trait of a ~~copy of the Book~~
                     Text. Work

---

it's thus an ideal absent leaf that gives rise to the vol of 384 p. (the 25th as me.

---

the mobile leaves are as fixed for me as for the crowd, which gives rise to the volumes

according to what precedes

113 (A)

2

| I exercise my right to read the book | for which payment is made by me to the assistants, in the sense that only I read the volume and seize ~~the volume~~ in |

Each place costs 500 f.   be it x 8 = 4000 f. to
                  diversely
each session, which is repeated 3 times = 12000 f
for each volume ~~printed in the same way~~ three times (each time
        (of these 4000) is mobile and diversifies
                          is worth 3, be it 3 f
with one of the 3 leaves as center of the 3) ~~= 12000 vol~~
and it's
~~as 4000 copies of each of the 3 editions~~
= 12000 f. that I have the right to earn.

of 12000 f at 12000 volumes
        each vol. at 1 f.
            — the 3 at 3 f

— I had 24 ~~listeners~~ dignitaries there (8 x 3 = 24)
        ~~and 72 including the guests (24 x 3 = 72)~~
              and I the 25th

or a ~~volume~~ volume —
copy — able to
mobilize and at 3 f

This operation takes place
to fix the price of the volume at 3 f, by
showing it to be triple — and its printing at 4000

3600? for
    costs

⌐I sell them myself in my lifetime as the 1st equipped, the time to prove
              that it's that —

This way, by summoning these 480 persons, to whom
8 and 3 times = 24)
I give a reading (by ~~24 and 3 times = 24~~) of <u>twenty</u> volumes,
which would be worth * 1000 francs from each one,
for nothing; I acquire the right to come into this
sum (of 480 thousand francs,) by publishing
the whole, be it
~~my Readings~~ in 480 thousand volumes at 1 f: ~~arranged~~
or as much of a thousand copies as of places; that arranged

as according to the Readings, namely ~~20 vol of 24 leaves (384 p)~~

---

* to establish that that is worth 1000 francs (the fact: that the crowd will buy)
reciprocal proof

** I x 3? 1440

115 (A)

or 4 plays of 5 l.

in 4 plays of 5 v.

20 v. each printed at 24000 cps. (be it per-
haps 8000 in each manner of the triple reading of the vol of 384,
— 24000)

---

which would cost anyone else a thousand francs — and me, I
prove it by giving a thousand francs, against the acquisition of the vol.
i.e. by settling for 480,000 f. to which the printing is reduced

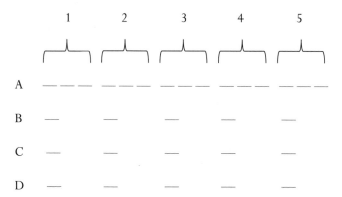

Pages
384 x 5 = 1920
x 3 = 5760
leaves
24 x 5 = 120
x 3 = 320

117 (A)

In this test of the crowd by the narrations or recipro-

cally

me, I'm outside it. just a reader carrying my copy
when read 3 times, having won it ⌐

≠   and to prove that I'm not the only one to read like this? — to read
of the crowd at this

each leaf successively costing 500 f. price of a
place. draw at 500, in the order it's in — and we

?

~~So, to give the reading this way~~   In short, these three
sessions of the same Reading in 3 different periods
of the year, it's to start over my Readings 3 times.

The Readings are composed for a year of 5 different
~~books~~ volumes, ~~thus~~ read ~~successively~~ simultaneously, over the course of
a week — which repeats itself 3 times ~~for~~ in 3
different periods of the year. = 24 places (or 72) x 5 = 120 (or 360)

$$= 4000 \text{ x } 3 = 1200 \text{ x } 5 = 60000 \text{ f}.$$
volumes and francs

indeed a crowd)
and 4 years = 480 dignitaries (x 3 = 1440 assistants. ~~crowd~~
(x 500 =)
240,000 vol and fr.

119 (A)
(3

   Such is the constitution of the <u>volume</u> (fixed in one session
          or 3
in this way the volume is mobile, triple in its reading: but this mo-
bility ~~o~~ only extends to one volume.
  the 5
   between different volumes of the same work, there
can be a prolongation of one by the 4 others,
~~according to~~ by establishing the relations between the corresponding parts
to these ones: ~~tha~~ that creates a sort
   sonorous
of game, of instrument
   but between the 4 fragments (1 . 2 . 3 . 4 . 5) of works
given annually, ~~there is no~~ in 4 ~~series of~~ Readings,
there is no relation, no link can
establish itself —

8 x 3 = 24 (384 p)

. . .   x 3

x 3

—   = = 72   10 times

—   x 5 = 360 leaves

—   and places

8 of 9

12 of 4   = 40 v of 9   = 400

60 of 6   for me.   vol.

or 10 cp.

printed at 10   for me

= 400 vol of 9   *places*

— my 40   *and leaves*

360 cps

121 (B)
(2

40 v. (9 f) or 1 cps. x 10 = 400 v.

360 copies are needed   or 10 cp.
x 40   but which are not
14400   given like this to the 360
to obtain 3 600 cp.   having no more than an annual relation
              + my 400   it's to print at 100
              = 4000

                                                    remains
at 100, 10 cps. of which I have   or 90

or (2

to sell my 10 copies
            various   manuscript

123 (B)
3

90 copies at 100 f.
                      the 40 v.
  be it 9000 f.

from the place to the session?   from the leaf (in 9) to the volume

2)

obtain 360 volumes

~~— my 40~~

be it 400

— my 40   or printing at

360 vol   10

9 of which remain

to be sold 1000 f.   and if not published for

my right to edit —   crowd

125 (B)

my 500   assistants..Chosen?
      francs
  1000 ~~persons~~

as soon as one charges 1000 f per place
no one will come
     so certainly obliged to invite
those who surround me most closely.
    I give 8000 each time

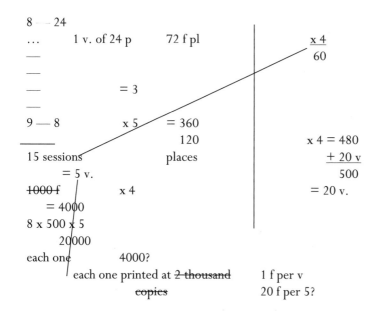

8 — 24
...   1 v. of 24 p   72 f pl   x 4
—   60
—
—   = 3
—
9 — 8   x 5   = 360
_____   120   x 4 = 480
15 sessions   places   + 20 v
       = 5 v.   500
~~1000 f~~   x 4   = 20 v.
    = 4000
8 x 500 x 5
     20000
each one   4000?
        each one printed at ~~2 thousand~~   1 f per v
                          ~~copies~~   20 f per 5?

127 (A)

each volume of 96 p (or 6 leaves ⌐ ⌐), there are 40 of them, to make a complete copy of the Book. There are ~~25~~ 24

(or 1000 — 40, threshold)

copies, be it 24 x 40 = ~~960~~ 960 volumes.

with minor differences, of lines

I have none; and successively   all. Full meaning?

I remove one as mine. That in
as many Sessions as there are volumes, namely
40: but 4 sessions reunited in one or 96 x 4 = 384
or 24 leaves, like 4 volumes reunited in
one (of 96 x 4 to 384): in 4 groups of six leaves,
in 4 groups of six assistants, 3 to 3. = 24 assistants

$$\begin{array}{r} 384 \\ 5 \\ \hline 1920 \end{array}$$

480 ^{places} 480 ^{leaves}

~~24~~ or 24 by   it could be that
sessions   volumes   no one but
     numbering   me — I take
          20   or 4   the 24 and then
     ~~(10 + 10)~~ (4 x 5)   x 5   a vol. me 25th
                                             in the name of the pure
                                                  leaf, glimmer

~~10~~   ~~10~~   ~~if written 5 times~~
~~double~~   ~~double~~   be it 96 (100) having the right to
~~sessions~~   ~~volumes~~   their 96. (+ 384) + 96 = 480
                                             and such for each group of 100
~~= 20~~   ~~= 20~~   = 2400 vol | 5 = 41
(for proof to be done)   ~~of the 20 v =~~
     that it's that   ~~= 9600~~
                                                 or 480 cp.
                                                 of 5 vol

          were I alone. to deny
          20 cps. of 24 l.   play
held here and there 10, 10
                         will
     (manuscript) or they   give the right to
                    copies
     a printing of 500, in which these 20 would take part.
     ~~and of which~~ 480 remain cp. which are fictive
               ~~the 20 v = 9600~~
               240 — 240   the 20 v
                         = 9600

                              nothing but to have put
                                   betrays me

129 (A)

places

~~guests~~ ~~listeners~~ leaves   *2 books* | *guests*   *leaves*

4 8 0   4 8 0   *one book, having* | *480*   *480*

                     ~~and at each one~~ a   *(1*

                     double interpretation

by 24 forming: *by 24*

a session equals a volume   *To establish a sort*   *a session equals a volume*

                     of competition —

       thus 20 sessions   *of series*   *thus 20 sessions*

                  10 + 10   *20 volumes*

       20 volumes   *doubl.*   identity of the

                      Book and the Play   *compose the reading*

or 4

sessions,

5 times 5 years]   *of the Book*

         compose the reading

96 places

and leaves   *the Book*

x 5   *the Play*

                  of the Book [thus ideal

         double   result of juxta-

——— form a copy ~~of the Play~~   position]   *or form a copy*

    and a performance of the Play.   ~~10 + 10~~   10 + 10

         double

So, me 1/25th,

~~In one sense as in the other~~

by this performance

I grant myself this double copy, the same and other,

Printing at 25   composed with self, to the double interpretation, and   *or 25*

which would seem to them, each one, in   *copies*

the Book

That, to start it over
once, if it takes
place there?

leaves, destiny, ~~[and free for them, on the~~ *Printing*

or not   *25*

outside, to buy, ~~here or there~~ *the 480*   *of the Book*

my 20

volumes (or 24 copies) which, with ~~mine,~~ *form my copy*

= 500 ~~[5 x 2 = 10 cp]~~ *volumes*

130 (A)

Each year 5 ~~times~~ years   100 sessions
At 2 f. per vol. or 20 f. per cp.
        9600 f.   100
                      sessions

        here and there ⌐| and |⌐   twice,
— there is no 25ᵗʰ 1/2 leaf — this is why I take, me 25ᵗʰ, the
        be it 48 1/2 l or 24 l.   is   absent
24 1/2 leaves existing, on which ~~are~~ interspaced the ~~pure~~ leaf (⌐| and |⌐)
                                1/2 f.   absent
and it's because of this (that I take these 48 or that the ~~pure~~ leaf only exists)
                            here and there   ten times
that the full printing takes place. (I sow, so to speak ~~this volume~~
            double volume   be it 10 x 48 = 480 volumes = ~~volumes~~
~~The time that~~ this entire ~~copy~~ — ~~so that there are 480 cop-~~
    ~~double or 480~~   ~~without~~
~~ies~~   ~~(from the copy to 20 volumes) or, with the~~
    ~~volumes~~   and multiplied by   4800 #
~~500 in all,~~ 10 ~~volumes~~ = ~~9600.~~) From the ~~void~~ leaf to
            sessions   absent
                      from 20 vol to
    ~~96~~4800 ~~copies~~ volumes.   (printing of 480,~~000 vol.~~)

Nothing emerges
but from the sessions

500

I say that there are not a ~~thousand~~
persons and if 480
not ~~a thousand or~~ 500
at best.　　　　challenge to make

come

the antagonism is
there in the way that this
edition, the only one, is bought
or printing at 500

from 480 to 4800 readings
to each one 1 or 10 volumes
only I find myself again with
two copies or 20 vol.
thus multiplied

---

each one having the right, by attending once, to the
totality if he desires it.　　I scatter that for them or others, once they
have returned into the crowd.

131 (A)

In short
instead of a leaf that each one would possess —— he will not have
it, ~~Ikee~~ me keeping the whole, but I'll have given him
the value of the 24 or of the audience's pooling
he'll have had his samples of $1/20^{th}$ of the wrk. and if he is interested
in possessing the whole, the totality of the Sessions (or only coming
as much as me (I give the example)   once, to this Banquet, Life)
that immediately makes a ~~r~~eproduction at 480 listeners
x 20 copies = 9600.   nothing, in the greatest
                                       extension emerges from the sessions,
                                       part of the voice, etc.
But at least to foresee
this case. that would have to be
for the exterior

enormous leap
of the leaf —— dance

and it would be necessary in order to satisfy this audience, on average — or that
        possess   it has appeared to him — he only has
each of them ~~have~~ the same thing as me as ~~will belong to him~~ —
~~be it~~ the right to that — ~~he~~ but won't he desire to have
attended all, be it the 20 sessions and to obtain that by ~~the~~ the Book,
total?   even in this enlargement,
exactly, and it's the press office. Thus nothing emerges from the Sessions —
~~25~~ 24 copies ~~will be~~ would certainly be necessary (not including mine)
of the double volume of the double session, that multiplied by the
20 sessions — ~~Be it~~ for the 20 volumes, be it 480 double
             20
copies (with my 500) Printing at 25.
                     of the total double copy or 20.
      But if each one wanted ~~to be represented~~ to have the whole
of the ~~Sess~~ Book a fragment of which he has attended, it
                $1/90^{th}$
would be necessary to multiply by 20.   (480 x 20 = 9600)

133 (A)
(2

extract the relation of the <u>leaf ~~to the copy~~ to the volume</u>
~~and in the same way as one, but~~   be it 480 leaves and 480 vol.
        arrangement of the leaf in the volume ~~24~~ according to 24

———————————————————————

        challenge that there be another than I
by reading, who buys the 20 ~~copies~~
vol. or

        the volume, I agree to make them print it and   to them,
if they complain that I whisper to them thus, ~~I~~ communicate it ~~to them~~
but at their request.

and it would be necessary in order to satisfy them ~~that there be~~, or that
       equal to me, of its appearance to him   relative to his session —
each one possess a double <u>copy</u> of the volume (instead of having
           a fragment $1/10^{th}$
attended the Reading and having the Book ideally, in short so that he'd
possess it and could consult it as needed) it would be necessarythat there be,
~~as many not 24~~ (25 double copies ~~of 2~~ of 20 vol. inlcuding
mine, 24 remain, which ~~would make~~ would only make the contingent of a
       the   or 480
Session, supposing ~~my~~ double copy printed at 25 — ~~but~~
    24   volumes, making
~~that that~~ multiplied by 20 sessions, or ~~500~~ 480 double copies,
each of 20 volumes, which I offer to the crowd   (whether this
is composed of guests or of the audience, who takes them) = 9600 ~~copies~~
volumes ~~of which~~ [of which 480 x 20 = 9600 vol, the 400 others
minus my own or 40,

they are representative. |

135 (A)

and I take 500 of them
each appears at 500 f.
without paying anything
in the sense that I read a tripled
copy

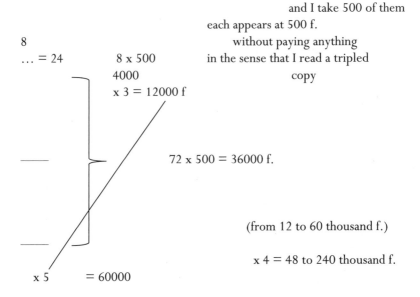

8
... = 24   8 x 500
                         4000
                         x 3 = 12000 f

72 x 500 = 36000 f.

(from 12 to 60 thousand f.)

x 4 = 48 to 240 thousand f.

x 5   = 60000

wrk
= 15 sessions x ~~3~~ 4 years = 60.

Thus to found everything on
a financial operation
— unbeknownst ~~to the~~ to the
                                guests
~~audience~~ — between people of the
                    world, but rich.

32   96   192

=

2 f. or 4 half-f. x 3 = 6 f. or 12 1/2 f.   12 f or 24 1/2 f

x 2

| | | | = 96 x 5 or 96 x 10

x 5 | |

= | |

160 ————   160 x 3 = 480   + 480

| |

       Sessions

| | = 5 ~~Read.~~   = 960

————   of 96 + 96

| |

            60 f.

| | 120 1/2

————   x 500

| | 60000 f.

| | =   10000

————   of 480 x 2

            at 3 f.

net 10000 f remain x 2

          = 20000

—————————————————————

x 2   = 40 v. of 96

          at 0.60

136 cont.

384 x 5   = 1920

= 24 f = 48 1/2 f.

x 2   =

240 f.
480 1/2 f.   480
                    x 500
         240000   ⌊3
                80,000 f net
              and start over
8 v. of 480 printed at
10,000 each.
= 80,000 at 3 f.

= 384 x 10 = 3840 (= 24 x 160)
+ 1/2 160 { 3 — 480
                  me
        = 320 x 12 1/2 mine

The 24 pers   from page to leaf
    x 40 = 960 pers.   x 2 = 480 l.
                                    2 cps.

     480 + 480   30 l + 30 l = 60 x 2 = 120 x 2 = 240
~~Verse~~

	1/2 Dr 1/2 Plays = 16 x 2 p
	480 + 480 = 320 x 3 = 960 p x 2 = 1920 x 2 = 3840
	1/2 Poems 1/2 Dr
~~Play~~	96 x (5 x 2 = 10) = 960 = 12 x 320
	= 48 x 2 =
~~Poem~~	480 + 480 = 96 x 20 x 2
	1/2 ball 1/2 motifs = 96 x 40
Parades	480 + 480 (or)
~~Stage~~	1/2 motifs 1/2 ball
ballets	

                         = 480 x 8 (2 cp. = 16)

~~Poems~~ Verse
~~Songs~~ Motifs
           480 + 480
      1/2 Myst 1/2 It's   = 480 x 6 = 2880 x 2 = 5760
              Pages   or 10 double Read
Myst   480 + 480
      1/2 It's 1/2 Myst ~~The 2 cps~~ 4 belonging x 10 sessions
song   Pages   ~~5 read.~~   ~~= 24 Read.~~
____   x 2
Articles Book   = 20 sessions or 10
It's   480 + 480   double Read.
    1/2 Song 1/2 Articles
             384 x 5 Series-market 10 cp of 484
     480 + 480   384 x 5 Sacrifice   x 2~~96~~ = 20
  1/2 Articles 1/2 Song   returned

of the Read
and of the printing
identity of the ~~of the session and of the volume~~   ~~in the year~~
place and the leaf   in the year, same
of the session and the volume ~~readings of 3 works~~   people

Read │ 4 places 4 leaves   ~~x 3 (development~~
     │   ~~of the leaf) = 12~~ ~~x 2 = 24 vol x 4 years~~
     │ x   development   ~~Read of 3 works~~   ~~24 sessions~~
     │ 5 of the leaf in 5   x 3 Sessions   x 2 =
     │ = 20 pl 20 leaves   5 Volumes   successive
                                  = 120 places
                                      and leaves

6 volumes printed 5 times at 2000 cp. = 60,000
6 sessions given 5 times at 2000 f (500 x 4) = 60,000
~~x 5 = 120 sessions~~

= 10000 f (x 3 x 2) = 60000   ~~or 24 vol. printed 5~~
(320) x 3 = ~~960~~ 60 leaves or 960 p. x 2 = 1920   or 3 double vol.
                                                printed 5 times
the 5 different times   3 double sessions given 5 times
if given in 320 each time   ~~at 1000 each = 2000 x 5 = 10000~~
of 1000 each = 10000 f   ~~4 x 500 f = 60,000~~
        at 2 f   4 Books
(1 f of which is for me)   x 4 years + 1 year
                                                of rest —
attain 480 places ──── — 480 leaves   and repeat.
                                              ~~indefinitely~~
= 24 sessions   24 volumes   ~~or 3 times~~
of 20 places   of 20 leaves
at 500 f =   at 500 cp. at 2 f   at   960.
240000 f =   = 240000 l ~~eps~~ leaves   480,000

(

        pure

financial operation
  through the book
      if not

        none

———

———————

    480 persons
  the 500

       me 20

Each one pays 500
   in case only —
      and if no one

        me

                this 2 times

later 900 l.

     after resting a year —

140 (A)

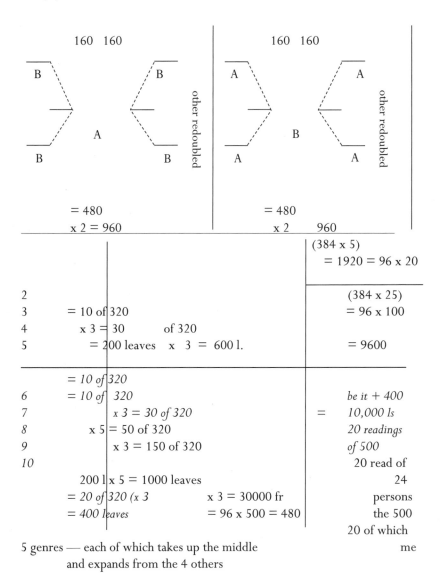

1

160   160   160   160

B   B   A   A

A   B

B   B   A   A

other redoubled   other redoubled

= 480   = 480
x 2 = 960   x 2   960

(384 x 5)
= 1920 = 96 x 20

2   (384 x 25)
3   = 10 of 320   = 96 x 100
4   x 3 = 30   of 320
5   = 200 leaves x 3 = 600 l.   = 9600

= 10 of 320
6   = 10 of 320   be it + 400
7   x 3 = 30 of 320   =   10,000 ls
8   x 5 = 50 of 320   20 readings
9   x 3 = 150 of 320   of 500
10   20 read of
                                        24
200 l x 5 = 1000 leaves   persons
= 20 of 320 (x 3   x 3 = 30000 fr   the 500
= 400 leaves   = 96 x 500 = 480   20 of which
                                          me

5 genres — each of which takes up the middle
and expands from the 4 others

It's this
Undo   to find something
~~Th~~   idea   that is not — <u>that</u>   sickness
             in the book
~~Self~~   its mechanism   ~~Myst~~
~~Dr~~   operator there
                                           ~~life~~
~~Th~~   ~~Myst~~   ~~party~~
~~Myst~~ ~~Self~~ ~~Dr~~   ~~the temple~~   ~~Hymn~~   ~~Idea~~   ~~indirect~~
                ~~hero~~   ~~Symbol~~   ~~the hymn Self~~
                ~~man~~   ~~hymn~~

                    ~~Myst~~   The mystery is
                    ~~Myst~~   already no longer —
                    Self   the Idea is there
                    Dr   visible there
                    — Myst   it's clean
             Th   ~~Hero~~   glimmer
                            the Year   in titles
~~The City~~   the city   ~~the crowd~~   transparence
             ~~the City~~   ~~the crowd~~
                      Read
             Hero
             ~~Symbol~~   Hymn   ~~Lives~~
             year   life
             man

~~Law~~   ~~Self~~   inspiration
~~being~~ ~~Idea~~   elimination and <u>law</u>   to make use
             white book   of what
             or <u>Idea</u>   law glimmer

141 a

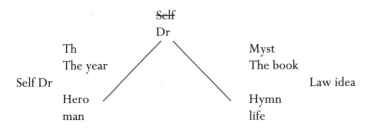

Apart from the homeland the people . this poetry that
nurtured our childhood —

143

1 session	one year	10 Read	4 years	4 ~~times~~

~~in this way~~

or 4 years
after

4 1/2 1 (= 32)   = 12 1/2 1 = 96 p   same thing   2nd Series   same day

⌐│ └   3 = _|_|_| |_|_|_ x 2 = 24 1/2 1 = 12 l. inverting = 96 x 4 = 24 f.
            |_|_|_   _|_|_| = 192 p.   = 384 p
└   ⌐   (to make them pay twice
    x   if = 2 f)
    5   exchange of the bottoms of 480   and 2 copies
    =
10 1/2 1 │   3 = 480   x 2 = 960
= 160 p │   = 96 x 5   = 96 x 10

                                │ one year 10 Read.
                                │ 5 before, 5 after the Day of the Year
            = 160 x 6   160 x 12 = 320 x 6   40 in
                                                        4 years
        = 500 l   100   40 times
4 half l 4 1/2 pl = 2 l = 2 pl = ~~500~~ x 2 = 2000 = 12 places   the 25th = 40 x 24
                            x 3   (doubles)   960

                        = 6000
                        x 2

20 of 384   = 12000 l   =
= 80 of 96   2 v   x 5
    printed at 10,000   = 60,000   x 2 = 120,000 l
                            —   net 60,000 f
    20000 cp at 3 l = 360   1 f. me   for the 2 f
                        1 f print
                        1 f false expenses
                            and
                            hotel

1000 f Per leaf

development of 2 leaves in 3

6 fr

4 1/2 f.   12 1/2 l (= 96 p)   48 1/2 l

= 4 1/2 pl. (= 500^f x 4 = 2000^f) x 3 =   x 4 =

             12 1/2 p (6000 f)   48 1/2 p

x 5   in 2 sessions

(here I show)   of the same ones (1000 f each)

= 20 1/2 f   to make of it   = 24 l. (384 p)

               = 384 x 5

= 10 f.   (3 f)   192 + 192

= 160   = 480 p x 4

           1920 p   = 320 x 6

               6000 x 4 = 24000   24 places of 1000

                      x 5   x 5

                     120000   120 places of 1000

blocks   = 360 pl.

6 v. from 320 to 2 l = 12 l each printed at 10000   x ~~5~~ 3

320 x 6 x 3 = 18 (9 + 9) ~~36 v of 320~~   and start over

384 x 5 x 3 = 15   ~~30   of 384 (15)~~   7 years

145 (A)

5 x 3 = 15
from page 15 to leaf 15

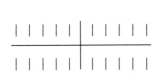

20 x 3 = 60

4 read. of 15 leaves
240 p.

x 6

= 120 x 3 = 360

= 24 read.

96 p x 20 = 1920

3840 ls

times 2 = 1920   3600 p.

division
into 3 leaves o

12 = 36 | | | | | | x 10

= 120 = 360

| | | | | |

x

3

= 360 = 1080

=

36 and 128

id

= 40 of 96

x 20 x 9

id 360

= 384 l. x 4 *3840 f.*

times 16 *160*

4000 f

xxxxxxxx

146 (A)

Thus to be published simultaneously:

A——Z̶ 384. I   and   384 X Z̶——A

which constitute the

t̶h̶e̶ two Genres   (which are only the Inverse)

— and keep going until X — f̶o̶r̶ in one direction

in the other until I

p̶r̶o̶b̶a̶b̶l̶y̶ ̶w̶i̶t̶h̶ ̶i̶n̶t̶e̶r̶s̶e̶c̶t̶i̶o̶n̶ ̶o̶f̶ ̶t̶h̶e̶ ̶t̶w̶o̶ ̶g̶e̶n̶r̶e̶s̶ ̶i̶n̶t̶o̶ ̶o̶n̶e̶ ̶a̶n̶o̶t̶h̶e̶r̶ ̶t̶o̶

f̶o̶r̶c̶e̶ ̶t̶h̶e̶ ̶w̶h̶o̶l̶e̶ ̶t̶o̶ ̶b̶e̶ ̶h̶a̶d̶

480   480

?

two <u>alternatives</u> of a same subject, — either this, or that —
(and not treated therefore, historically — but
always intelluectually,

divided into 10
this ~~div~~ which   will reunite by 4, to collect, divided into 10,
a sample in each ~~one~~ and form a symphony
(or vol of 384)

thus represents (not by the genres, but) the totality
of a poem in which $1/10^{\text{th}}$ form $1/4$ of symphony, it

148 (A)

384 x 10
————————

There are only <u>two genres</u>
published as <u>book</u>, as   x 2
this is.

namely ~~respectively~~

but since that conceals a theater *, one must
recover in it (is it by arranging the book otherwise) the two
parts of Th —

All of modernity is produced by a reader. The hat — etc.

———————————————————————————————————

* thus you pay double for the book

theater to play outside self

= 96 x 40 (3840)
x 2

40 double readings
to 24 persons
= 960 persons

150 (B)

in short 480 — 480   960
                                    x 2 =
              480 — 480   1920

id

4 being determined at 2 = 8 in 2
and being composed of 2 each

book

newspaper

Keys.   year

at

cloister   verse

day

city

newspaper

or

Idea   figure

Dr   verse

152 (A) (1)

480	•	480	
= 80 x 6	•	=	80 x 6

(here concerning 2 series of leaves album)
5 of which are necessary. to form these 6 parts

The thing presents itself. as 25 leaves or 384
p. like this

A   B

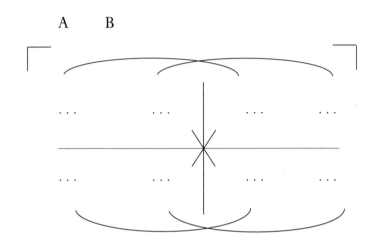

and

384 ls. plus 1 l.
or 8 leaflets cut
in 3 for cards
= 24 listeners

first start by throwing half of the edition and
come to resume this way — ~~then~~ the pages left open as such on the table —
reintegrate them into an album
into an album — that 1st reading; then 2nd reading,
as a book, and 2nd half of edition —

154 (A) (3)

it's
                    (A and B) *
            ~~the intersection of~~ two poems, simultaneously
~~published~~ given

        384 here, or middle term, ~~thus doesn't exist~~
[between 480 + 480 ~~x 2 =~~ (= 960) x 2 = 1920] and contents
5 times — or 5 ensembles of 384, volumes — in 1920,
forming a whole ** = 96 x 20. It's the volume and

---

* doubtless the one initial, the other final
                                    thus clean stop at X

** there are 4 series of 1920   = 7680
                                      + 320 = 8000

vulgar

just as it presents itself to the audience — or from out of the poem
of 480 + 480 (representing the manuscript) — part of
that, readable as ~~that~~ such, until exhaustion
of the 5 — and arranging themselves ~~in pages~~ in album leaflets —*

— There are thus 5 readings in one direction.
arrangement
from the vulgar book to the album — and 5 in the other
manuscript
direction. from the album or manuscript to the book,

folding. Be it 10, double readings *

---

* in short there is a second reading for the initiated.

---

* and 4 times. or 40 — with 20 volumes of 384

156 (A) (5)

these 480 — 480.
~~repres~~ are, as for them — a complete original poem.
which ~~mixed~~ united with another equal —
divides into pieces of 96 x 4
so as to form 20 of 96 or 5 of 384.

they number 8 ——————————

    composing
    ~~and while forming~~ 4 ensembles

perhaps with
double repetition
of the same text —

only 2 of which
we give perhaps?

or, if th

and myst.

Dr   hymn

hero

and this is how they are formed
    30   —   30
or namely
    3 x 10 + 3 x 10
or the same triple leaf for the voice, intonation —
~~in which alone the same text can continue.~~
until equality 10. That is, continuity of the same

text. That ~~and~~⌐ and ⌐. The same text

Are the two inverse subjects ⌐ and ⌐ or rather   <u>480 — 480</u>
                  480 — 480

158 (A)
6

can thus continue through 10 leaves ⌐ and 10

leaves ¬ (echo, purity) be it 320.
   and 480 is nothing else than 320 type
  x 3 (x 8 = 24 + 1/25th cards in white

            role, partition.

  dissimulated this way in $\dfrac{480 + 480}{480 + 480}$

   and even more in 384 x 5
     or 96 x 4 x 5

2 leaves ⌈ and ⌉ once separated exchange
their 1/2 interior leaf
the same thing takes place for 2 other leaves exchang-
ing their 1/2 exterior leaf.
The exchange is complete and necessitates 4 leaves — be it 64 ls,
in 32 + 32, 2 1 + 2 1   example

⌈ deployment in an album

I take one of the tripled
leaves of each no. 1 —
⌈ with ⌉   or corresponding
    naturally,   two
of the ~~four~~ poems constituting here
each one a fragment of 96;
~~a symphony of 384, for~~
~~ac according to~~; and act thus with
the 3: while juxtaposing —

160 (A)

2

then the same thing to be done inversely, i.e.
beginning and ending inversely for the other double
fragment of 96 — of the whole forming the 384.
    in this way I reduce this 384 that presents itself in book leaves
in this state of partition [from probable Dr to hymn]

⌈ and this is what
| I do in Read ⌋

The <u>Hero</u> extracts the Hymn from the Dr.   this is the operation
        in Mystery (Th. Idea)

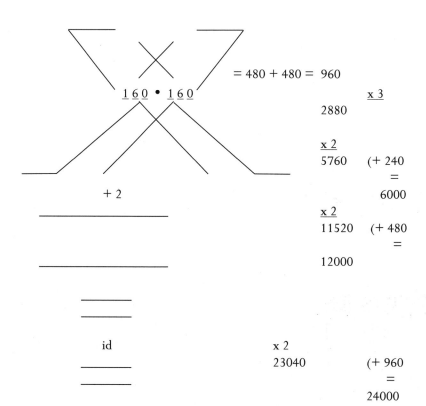

= 480 + 480 = 960

$\underline{1\ 6\ 0}$ • $\underline{1\ 6\ 0}$

x 3

2880

x 2
5760   (+ 240
=
6000

x 2
11520   (+ 480
=
12000

+ 2

id

x 2
23040   (+ 960
=
24000

162 (A)
(2

$$= 96 \quad \cancel{96 \times 96} \qquad \cancel{72000} \qquad \underline{24000}$$

$$\dots \times 10 \dots \times 10 \qquad \cancel{3} \qquad 3$$

$$480 - 480 \qquad \qquad =$$

96 x 10   960 $\cancel{720\ B}$ 8000

x 3   x 2   7690   or 500 leaves

= 96 x 30   1920

x 2   =   (+ 320)   (x 3 = 1500

= 96 x 60   384 x 5 (x 3

= 15)

_____

x 4

= 384 x 60

4 times. 4 series
of Readings
and two ~~works~~ at once
genres

320 = ⌐ ⌐ x 10)   (of 320 x 3 or 960)
               8 ~~x 3~~ = 24   24 given in 20
    8   of 320   of 384

                                                           Iliad
of 320 x 3 (= 960   or 12 + 12   Odyssey
      given in   (60 leaves 30 + 30)   of 320   modern
roles   480 + 480   with exchange?   implying
8 = Dr   plays.
4 Dr   ~~and divided into~~   48   48
or Symph.   Be it ⌐ ⌐ ⌐   ⌐ ⌐ ⌐
                                     . .
12   x 10   x 10
and that doubles   = 96
             x 10   and this 4 times for 4 parts
                  = 96 x 4
                    = 384   (x 10 =
3840)

                                                x 2
     going together
     be it 384 x 10

                      96 x 3 or ⌐ • ⌐ a leaf x
                      multiplied by 3 different concurrents,
     + 384 x 10   notations
8 persons
      =
   960 x 8
  = 7680 (+ 320 = 8000) = 16 x 500   10 v. of 384

164 (B)

384
   x 20

+ 320 p
_____

      invitations
          or 2 leaves
   x 3
   = 480

and start over

from 320 x 24 to 384 x 20

3 states

480 — 480   x 8
in the block state   (middle)

giving

320 x 3   dr.
x 4   roles x 2
                                  symph.

— and a book
96 x 10
x 4 ~~x 4 x 3~~   x 2
= 384

                                          • book

166 (A)

~~123D.E times 5~~ = 160 x 3 = 10 f x 3 = 30 f.   I II III IV etc. X
~~A B C A B C~~
          ~~D E~~
~~2nd leaf~~   = 48 x 2)   I
~~A+A+A+A+A~~   480 = 96 (= 16 x 3 + ~~2 x 24~~) x 5

        8 of 480
        or 40 of 96

        480 = 96 x 5
        = 15 x 8 = 120 f.]

                        one leaf in 3 = 48 (x 2 = 96)

                        thus
                        — 3 editions of the whole
                              the same ones

                        be it 120000 f
                              x 3
                              36000 f

3 editions   of each

   there   leaf   1 f author

                              and 1 f bookseller

                                    2 f each vol

<u>480</u>   <u>480</u>

48 x 10

     96 | 96

                            = 10 f

     ——————

     96 | 96

<u>480</u>   <u>480</u>   <u>times 2</u>

  = 384   = 480 x 8

                                  = 3840

  x 5   = 384 x 10.

  = 1920

24 f x 5 = 120 f. x 2 = 240 ~~x~~ f.

                    240 x   ~~the 24000 f~~

                    500 f per l.   ~~remain~~

                    <u>= 48000</u>   ~~for me~~

                    120000

166-167 a

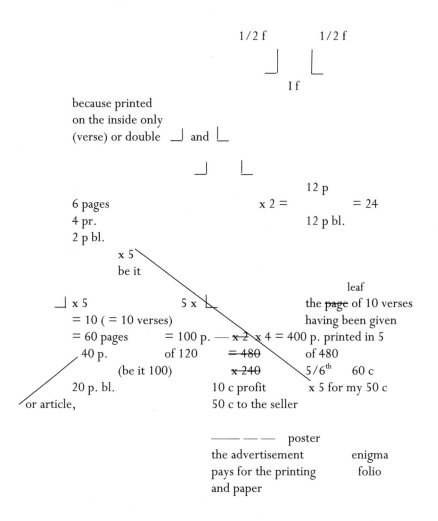

1/2 f   1/2 f

⌐ ⌐

I f

because printed
on the inside only
(verse) or double ⌐ and ⌐

⌐   ⌐

12 p

6 pages   x 2 =   = 24
4 pr.   12 p bl.
2 p bl.

x 5
be it

leaf

⌐ x 5   5 x ⌐   the ~~page~~ of 10 verses
= 10 (= 10 verses)   having been given
= 60 pages   = 100 p. — ~~x 2~~ x 4 = 400 p. printed in 5
40 p.   of 120   ~~= 480~~   of 480
(be it 100)   ~~x 240~~   5/6th 60 c
20 p. bl.   10 c profit   x 5 for my 50 c
or article,   50 c to the seller

——— — — poster
the advertisement   enigma
pays for the printing   folio
and paper

hunt   yacht   funeral   baptism

    war   wedding —
    —   war
                                           ~~wa~~
~~ball~~ —   ~~meal~~   bomb
                                           theft
ball   meal   desert   firewrk.

168 *a*

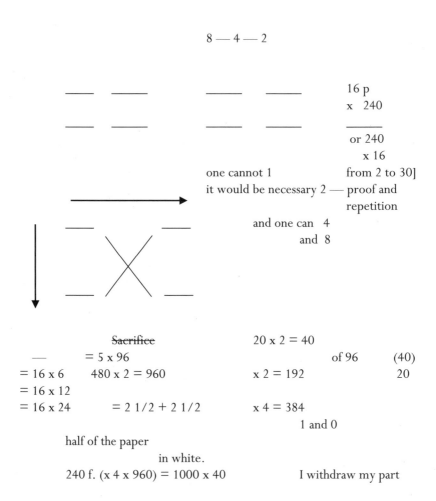

8 — 4 — 2

16 p
x 240

or 240
x 16

one cannot 1   from 2 to 30]
it would be necessary 2 — proof and
                                                 repetition

and one can 4
and 8

~~Sacrifice~~   20 x 2 = 40
—   = 5 x 96   of 96   (40)
= 16 x 6   480 x 2 = 960   x 2 = 192   20
= 16 x 12
= 16 x 24   = 2 1/2 + 2 1/2   x 4 = 384
                                                                1 and 0

half of the paper
in white.
240 f. (x 4 x 960) = 1000 x 40   I withdraw my part

He finds himself in a City-place-where   he could have
                                          celebrated — (wedding vows)
                                    Th   Dr
The exploit that should have brought him glory   is a crime: he stops in

time in this Operation; of which it's a miracle that the Invitation he understood
so well is enough for the lady who made it to him unknowingly perhaps.
                                                                glimmer

of the one who inspired it   genius . farce

                              but to leave the Invitation without responding to it
                                        order
and that the woman had been afraid of what   should it be No —
she did to him. Unknowingly   while she has given herself to him to this degree
perhaps. Agrees. hat   one cannot —
        he conceals her   is a theft. gun - taken
                in self

                                        operation | which is not

169 (A) cont.

———

path
hospital
market   Invitation to <u>party</u>   Operation
torture   to everything except the <u>meal</u>   If there is one
gift —   law it's that one
advertisement   since we'd die
~~simple choice~~   without eating
decoration
——   thus his hunger. The law keeps quiet
                                    eats —   sermon?
        doesn't dare show itself this way
                                    it veils itself   crime   (~~division~~
                                    in satin
                                    is neither gun. which is neither — nor —
Be it   to eat the lady
    at (let's suppose)   20 f. for her   advertisement   suffrage

hunt   yacht   funeral   wedding   baptism
                                    place   decoration   collapse
                                    City what is it? prison   torture
ball.   firewrk   in
                        factory | school
                                            |
factory   school   prison

                but… we could
                never have known what —   it's
                satin — hat explodes   clear
                                    sun   as
                                                    day

double   double place instead

each Read. session   — and doubles in printing

12   place and time

~~24~~ double places

as if No one —   outside

is   the same here and there, frame and stability

~~and I 1 (/25th) am there~~   not 13th, 25th

and the reader

(which is enough)   and naturally I'll come back

removing ~~the~~   12 times (to return that) 12 Read. being Self

~~part of all or~~ the ensemble here   successively these 12 here representative

places   of the totality

or 1 part, which has no direct relation with [be it 20 leaves at 1 f

No one   their number

knows   present or not, but with the fictive   according to 2 series

anything   price   20 fr x 12 = 240 f I spend   *this twice*

= 12 Read. being self,   of the Invitation   the double reading   *or 240 x 2 = 480*

successively these 12   but rests   = 480 f I spend,   *or 500 — 20*

here representative of the   on the price   or 500 f —   *(— my place*

totality   of invitation   my place

20 taken

as unity = the play

~~the play~~

as well as me   12 =

480 per play

resting   hat   4 times

on the price of Read: x 3 for 3 wrk

20 f.   the 3 blows

in the opposite direction

everything remains redistributed

20 v. of 25 fe   = 5 f for the whole

x 4 = 20 f

of which 1 f. per person

0.05 c over 0. 25 c

or 0.01 c. over 0.05

printing is infinity

171 (A)
(1

Play
or
~~this dr~~ this performance with concert
poem
dialogue ~~stage~~ and symphony
for stage and orch
— occupies the ground of the Wrk —

verse

and as published in a book
newspaper and verse
adapts — to a regular newspaper
once and for all, ~~reducing~~ and,
~~every~~ all the questions answered,
by someone who has reduced them in his
hat ⌐   way of making everything
virginal — which is exte-
rior to the poem

— and as a publication

~~instead of performance~~
it is, by fragments   of

the performance — each one giving it
the   rhythm
~~an~~ ensemble — according to its fraction

⌐ Which is — be it 1 / 8th?]

173 (A)

(1

Book,

The four volumes are one ~~of them,~~ the same, ~~repeated twice~~

presented twice as its two halves,

first of the one and last of the other juxtaposed to

last and first of the one and of the other: and little by

with the help

little its unity reveals itself, of this work of comparison

showing that this makes a whole

in two different directions, as a fifth

part, formed from the ensemble of these four fragments,

apparent or two repeated:	*5 leaves*	. . . . .	. . . . .	*= 20*
this will thus take place 5 times		. . . . .	. . . . .	*= 320*
or 20 fragments grouped				
in 2 ~~of~~ 10, found identical	*(25)*		*x 5*	*= 1600*
by	*we have 10 leaves*			*320*
				x 5
	plus 10 leaves = 20			*100 leaves*

be it annual, with ~~96~~
96 places, 96 leaves
for 100 if I'm 25th without
a place or a leaf — I had ~~some of~~
them. (24 x 4 = 96. 25 x 4 = 100)

They are made in two days
at two per days: in
one year; and last for
five years.

~~They correspond~~

175 (A)
3

              We thus have 4 volumes, 5 times.
i.e. once (quadrige) the 4   or to begin
first volumes, ~~and thus~~   with the middle
              concurrently,
~~following until~~   of the four
    books
~~works~~ which are each in
five volumes: and thus following,
~~until the exhaustion of the whole~~, as
                    Play
one ~~Play~~ quadruple ~~in~~ juxtaposed
in
five acts, ~~or sessions,~~ until the exhau-
stion of the whole. While meanwhile it
becomes manifest ~~tha~~ that these are four

books (of four concurrents)

Each in 5 volumes.

Thus 20 volumes | one volume per session
    20 sessions
      Readings   each volumes
  4 ~~Books~~ in five ~~Readings~~, years
              times
      Performances
  4 ~~groups~~ concurrently, each in five times

     and
480 places,   480 leaves.

177 (A)
5

I thus grant myself e̶a̶e̶ to each

Interpretation	Book
Performance	~~Volume~~

	12	12
	places 2	leaves 2
	assistants	1 / 2 leaves

480 places   480 leaves
          by 24 : or
one session equals one volume

                                          be it 10 sessions and 10 volumes

          The 25th leaf missing   double   repeated
and I presenting myself 25th = 20 sessions
and taking the 24: between   20 volumes
which I establish a relation
and which I <u>bind</u> into a volume
~~equaling 10~~ on which this
absent leaf is developed

The sessions go 4 by 4
and form as such an ensemble

179 (A)
2

Otherwise and if we published this way
~~in~~ by simultaneous halves ~~of~~
         there would be ~~in a case~~
nothing ~~but~~   ~~of possible~~ for the same
                   of existing
people, readings — but two parts
of the Wrk

                    — It is only by virtue of two repeated
texts that we can delight in a
whole part
                              or by virtue
                         of the turnaround
                         of the same text ~~in two~~
           — in a second way
              of rereading
                         which allows us to have
                   the whole
                         successively.

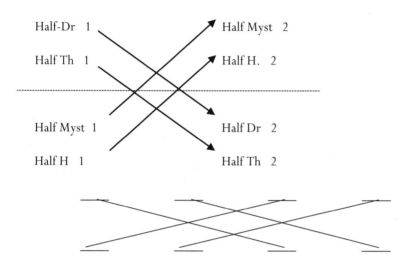

In this way 2 states of the Wrk. which complete one another,
each of
~~neither~~ of the two being only a half
made of 4 halves the 4 other
halves of which are in the other
          but each containing 1 complete
text of the Wrk.   repeated twice because
one part

181 (A)

a book neither begins nor ends: at most it
pretends

———

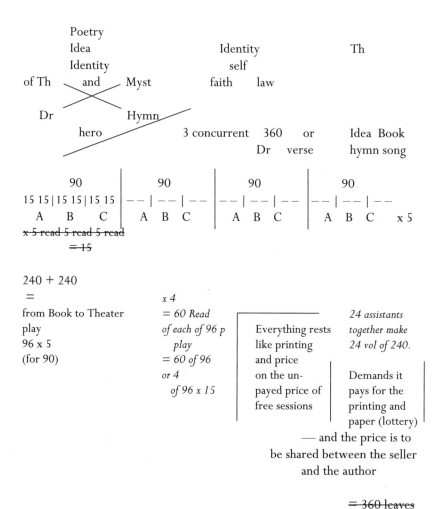

Poetry
Idea   Identity   Th
Identity   self
of Th   and   Myst   faith   law

Dr   Hymn
hero   3 concurrent   360   or   Idea Book
                               Dr   verse   hymn song

     90   90   90   90
15 15 | 15 15 | 15 15   — — | — — | — —   — — | — — | — —   — — | — — | — —
   A   B   C   A   B   C   A   B   C   A   B   C   x 5
x 5 read 5 read 5 read
      = 15

240 + 240
    =   x 4
from Book to Theater   = 60 Read   24 assistants
play   of each of 96 p   together make
96 x 5   play   24 vol of 240.
(for 90)   = 60 of 96   Everything rests
                              or 4   like printing   Demands it
                                 of 96 x 15 and price   pays for the
                                             on the un-   printing and
                                             payed price of paper (lottery)
                                             free sessions
                              — and the price is to
                           be shared between the seller
                                 and the author

                                   = 360 leaves

182 cont.

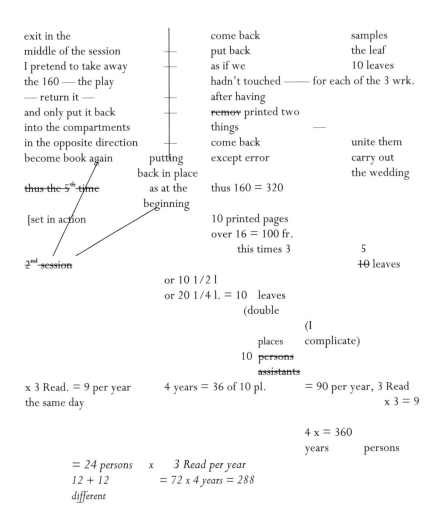

exit in the
middle of the session
I pretend to take away
the 160 — the play
— return it —
and only put it back
into the compartments
in the opposite direction
become book again

~~thus the 5th time~~

[set in action

~~2nd session~~

come back
put back
as if we
hadn't touched —
after having
~~remov~~ printed two
things
come back
except error

putting
back in place
as at the
beginning

thus 160 = 320

10 printed pages
over 16 = 100 fr.
this times 3

or 10 1/2 l
or 20 1/4 l. = 10   leaves
(double

places
10 ~~persons~~
~~assistants~~

samples
the leaf
10 leaves
for each of the 3 wrk.

—

unite them
carry out
the wedding

5
~~10~~ leaves

(I
complicate)

x 3 Read. = 9 per year
the same day

4 years = 36 of 10 pl.

= 90 per year, 3 Read
x 3 = 9

4 x = 360
years   persons

= 24 persons   x   *3 Read per year*
12 + 12   *= 72 x 4 years = 288*
different

seasons

3 days per year]————————————— the 3 annual read.

and make   (the credit

the 3   has already

3 read. per day   on the same day   taken place

which contains them   3 months

36 pl. x 4 = 144 crowd   already in essence   same day

12 x 12 —   and each sample   3.

of 5 forms in one   1920

season. the 1/3   2 000

of a vol of 240 —   240 — 240

already represented here   the ensemble

= 480

x 4 seasons

183 (A)

… … … … …

… … … … …

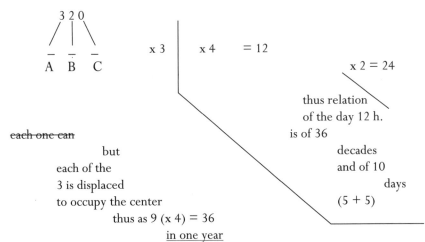

3 2 0

A   B   C

x 3 | x 4 | = 12

x 2 = 24

thus relation
of the day 12 h.
is of 36

~~each one can~~

but
each of the
3 is displaced
to occupy the center
thus as 9 (x 4) = 36

in one year

(1 is triple, the wrk. is published
to the third,

| x each time)

decades
and of 10
days
(5 + 5)

this gives
5 read of
96

and it's by virtue of the fact that
the vol triples in this way as a leaf
is printed on 3 (or 6
half leaves) recovering its
paper. (we have: 1 leaf =
96 pages [thus 72 printed]
and, if we give a sample
of the 5 works we have 96 x 5 = 480 or
72 x 5 = 360   play and year

according to the 3
dispositions
of 320
— in the 480 + 480
= 15

x 4 = 60
of 96
5 or 4 with 20

16 = 12 — 12 = 24

1/2 leaves in 5. 1 f. in 5 (folding in 8 = 6 x 2 = 12 x 2 = 24

~~or 10 1/2 f.~~

or the ensemble = 120 pages $\Big|$ (x 3 = 360)
of 160 $\Big|$ of 480

5 · 5 · 5   · · ·   (or 3/4)

A   B   C   · · ·

       5 · 5 · 5

       A   B   C   id = 6   i.e. another cp

   3   sessions   gained, from the right

sessions | samples   per year   that doubles reading,

A /. . .   to reverse

B /. . . .   here and that's all

C /. . . .   to the other session.

      | *this times 4* | | *that times 4* |

                  ?

A . . + . . =   320   (with echoes)

                                  identity of

B   320   id.   380 and self —

                                  160 to double

C   320   id.   reading —

                                  here and there

184 (A) cont.

or 240 over 320 x 3)

such an ensemble of 960 (or over 720)

x 2 1920

that times 2

320 + 320 + 320
~~320 + 320 + 320~~

identity of the
number of printed
pages

240 over

~~That~~ complete session ~~times~~   320

The session is composed of 2 Read. (x 2 = 4)   or 12 Readings   and the 240

3 sessions or 6 half sessions

per year   be it hunt-yacht   where a half

I hold them in my hand   because of the dis-   is presented

as 160, let us try the _| and |_   /positions of the 1/25th of   — — —

or 5 leaves, having managed to read them — leave —   leaves and vice versa

and return with another Reading, and redistribute them inversely

of \ in /

1 leaf in 5 l or or 10 half l.
reunite them into ⌐ ⌐

A   B   A   B
....

     A   B | A   B
    .... | ....

     2   x 2
  sessions   = 4 sessions

A .   160 + 160 = 320
B .   160 + 160 = 320

             320 x 5 = 1600
    this times 5 = 320 x 5 = 1600

                  3200
          over which
             1200 x 2
            = 2400 p.

4 sessions
of 24 seats   = 96   ~~this times 2 = 9~~
         and me 25th times 4 = 100 seats

= 2 cp.
                    320 − 320 − 320 − 320 − 320
     of the same = {
placed differently   320 − 320 − 320 − 320 − 320

186 (A)

72 seats

~~per year~~   in one session

or   12 x 6
~~(each of 2 persons~~
x 2 = 144 (12 x 12) or crowd   per year
        ——   ——

(seats

12		72	72
x 3	x 2	4	5
36	72	288	360

32
15

160	x times 2
32	= 144 s.

480

12

~~x times 4~~

=

188 (A)

3 sessions

is it not necessary
that the same ones be able
to hear the three?

or one among them
— is enough —

me

of one 3.
3
3

= 9

they the passersby.

24 guests
me 25th
in 24 sessions
so that these
24 have
each time
been, in my
24 appearances.

24
24

96
x 6
600
576

24)

is it in exchange for what is half-
white (the black writing — only find-
ing itself while below — in 1/2 cl)　　　　　　　　that

.. ./
　　./ ..　　　　　I show double subject
　　　　　　　　　　produced by this writing.

　the two series in the 1/2 l. are already to
bring the rhyme into the echo of two verses
　　　　　　— and the other half leaf —
　　　　　　　　　　　　　half or
　　　　　　　　　　　　　　　leaf
　　　　　　　　the stanza and the leaf

⌐ gilding
on 3 half leaves
at once.
　　　　with other book　　　　　／ we only prove in regard to
figure out straight away　　　　／　　　　　　　　others
gives the right to possess　and prove by reading

190 (A)

there are 8 pages
— 2 leaves —

Threshold the leaf counts.
makes the unity.
The leaf and the verse
The volume and the play

the page:
the sign —
   this book
abstracts itself

——

1/2 f.
the leaf
   1/4 of
= 2 ~~half~~ 1.

that can be tripled
on both sides

gesture   self
   page
page   ~~song~~
  hymn

and a double
in the whole leaf   3 1/2 1   +   3 1/2 1
or 4 quarters   or 6 1/4 of l   or 6 1/4 of l

. . .   . . .

. . . . . .

and renew it 4 times   . . . . . .
$96 \times 4 = 384$ . . .   . . .

~~and triple once~~   ~~384 x 3 = 1152~~
the inverse
then ~~the opposite~~

and the whole times $5 = 384 \times 10$
$5 + 5$

It represented one of the ~~leaves~~flets. — or the
12 seats the twelve leaves   (leaflets that we
cannot separate from leaves except to
insert them through an exchange and that's all)

⌈ purity electr light —
                          — the volume, despite the fixed
printing, becomes by this game, mobile
— out of death it becomes life ⌋

So that all that is there in a block —
happens there. 5 readings are necessary, be it 96 x
$5 = 480 \times 2 = 960$ ᵖᵃᵍᵉˢ (with 480)
                          double price.
                          establishment of the price
                                    ⌈ and the 100 f ⌋

—

A second series of readings can be given in the

opposite direction ↗   then ↘

192 (A)

this time return of the operator
relating the volume thus composed —

xxxxxxxxxxxxxxxxxxxxxxxxxxxxxxxxxxxxxxxxxxxxxxxxx

i.e.
an inverse operation

done relatively to the
second part of the audience. He will
read it ~~and~~ thus and will redistribute it to the
compartments but inverse   ~~like a~~

⎸ ⎸ ⎸ ⎸ ⎸

—————

—————

—————

—————

—————

⎸ ⎸ ⎸ ⎸ ⎸

⌐where it seems
— Such is the double session.
having shown the identity of this volume with
   self   and the
~~himself~~: it encompassed 24 persons —
each one having at one point

thus
~~his right and an equal, below, which he holds in~~
by half
in each of his hands, the time it takes to ~~bring them~~
those
~~into confrontation~~ join them together, ~~the~~ reversed corrected, like
but ⌊ if the others ⌋
the first — as if he confronted their
granted.
total format.

At this point he has ~~the~~ a number
of leaflets equal to half the seats in
the audience. be it 6, and in the same way as these
seats ~~take~~ are double, although
particularly for a dignitary, the leaves di-
vide into two leaflets.   [each leaflet
one of which is interior.
is 8 pages long — and 3 leaflets = 24 pages⌋
He shows this, changing
~~He reunites 3 leaves~~ ~~He changes the 3 leaflets,~~
~~,showing this:~~
~~leaf to leaf~~ the interior leaflet of the one to
the other leaf   be it the first ones ~~in two~~
two, the second and third twos

194 (A)

momentarily placed aside, <u>reads</u>.

    ⌐at least turning around three times
toward the left. (smile — wait patiently) to whom this successive
act appears more clearly — a bit veiled for the right
      he takes the leaves successively. ⌐

~~He always~~   until the moment
when the whole attained, the operator, ~~goes~~ rushes
straight in front of him, so that he comes, carrying
      identifying himself with it
(toward the voice that read) this booklet as
      for each one.
to him   ~~(identifying himself with it,~~

     The whole has lasted three quarters of an hour — a
quarter-hour interval (timbre of
     as it had been of waiting at the beginning
new, glimmer)
        and
                   ⌐total 2 h

The seats —— The furniture.
                              curtain
                  enters, by the space left empty by the seats
The reader ~~arrives salutes to the right, with a~~
at right and at left, and goes directly
~~glance, observes six places, even double.~~
     a bit bent over
~~turns arou~~ goes in ~~leaflet~~ to the furniture —— of lacquer ——
~~which divide this way~~   obviously half full
                                            in a diagonal.

          | | | | | as follows
          ———

               ———

                    ———

                         ———

                              ———
                                   | | | | |

each of these 6 compartments in a diagonal,
containing 5 leaves (number easily visi-
ble to the eyes) —— [the higher ones upright
                              He knows, then, and
                              a turn taken to what is
and the lower ones reversed?   ~~He takes one~~
                                   having become his right,
               turned toward where he came from, ~~on by the left~~
takes his place, under the single electric lamp, after having
first leaf ~~of the 1ˢᵗ comp~~ of the five ~~of the first~~
taken one   of each
compartment, high up —— ~~then turned toward the right~~
                         and low down, holding these
                         six leaves

196 (A)

price of the ticket

from 20 f

to ~~20 cents~~ 1 f = 20 cp. at 1 f.

6 places   120 cp.   10

20 f x 6 = 120 f   twelv.

                                            x 5

                                            ___

                                            600   50 twelv

                        x 2   =   100 twelv

                                                                   or 1200 f.

$$\frac{5}{5}$$

$= 5 \text{ x}$

198 (A)

in

What must be ~~on~~ one 1 / 2 l.

is ~~on~~ 5 half leaves — ⌟ and ⌊ , thus

on   on

~~which~~ 1 leaf is ~~in~~ 5 leaves —

absent

⌈ the 6th above

from 5 to 6.   ~~30~~

~~(from 12 to 50~~

~~year — play~~

= 160 p (or 120)

~~xxx~~ times 3 (3 sessions) = 480 p (or 360)

or 3 leaves in 15 (= 32 x 15 = 480)

8 forms, or genres
each of 3 vol of 320   = 24

3 vol of 320
= 960 (480 + 480)
       only half published
     = 480
         x 8

(240 + 240

<<
    from
    time to gold
from 12 to 20

200 (A)

A. 3 leaves, each one the 1st of the 1st volume of each
of the three parts

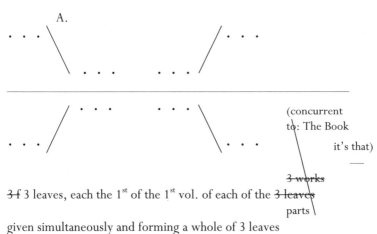

(concurrent
to: The Book
it's that)

——

~~3 f~~ 3 leaves, each the 1ˢᵗ of the 1ˢᵗ vol. of each of the ~~3 leaves~~

given simultaneously and forming a whole of 3 leaves
6 half leaves, 12 ~~1/4 of~~ quarter leaves: i.e. a
        simultaneous   between them
new way of reading ~~what is~~, these 3 l. offering
communications ~~between them~~ and the most prolonged,
(and demonstrate that these 3 concurrent works are the same, and of the same)
what otherwise, to the successive volume, would pre-
        meaning
sent no, any leaves added — or,
                which does not concern me and
                which I neither ~~kno~~ recognize nor
            one   assume
would present a false by chance — be it
the vol. as block, or old and contemporary way of reading.
~~reading.~~

error of the crowd	denounced by a thief who will tell the judge what I've done

That would repeat itself as many times as this theft.

for whose meaning

(for which I am not responsible — not signed such.

so much that I don't present myself to read differently

the I, if no one

or assume it   and it's that, clearly)

as many leaves as this this vol. contains, be it 5   in   \ / = 20

(5 x 4) or vol of 320 *,   3 times, as   / \

the three   240 + 240:

that 1st vol. of the 3 parts   (= 60 l. 480 + 480 (x 2)

*fictive, not existing as such   = 960

or not given as such, alone.

of 20 f

but triple

and we have   and by reduplication   5 being the leaf

3 f x 4 12 f   being   begun again in 5

(96)   which

= 384 x 5   = (1920)   isn't (6th)

or   or

126   60 f   320 thus gives

(12 x 5)   1 leaf in f begun again

over 5 in its

first   each

be it   of its two readings

(turnaround of the paper

—   384   maximum   thus the vol can only exist halfway;

5 —   simultaneity   plus the same thing of the other Wrk.

—   x 5   (concurrent. The Book

—   it's that

thus the possibility of inserting

newspaper

— advertisement

this and a second time   the verse existing in itself —

202 (A)
(4

In this way   24 Read assistants
                     x 4
                        = 96 per year. and I the 4 twenty-fifths
                                 = 1000
I keep.   4 triple volumes

_____

4000, printing x 4 = 16000 copies x 3 at 1 f = 48000 cp.
3 f. per vol. = 12000 x 4 = 48000 f

_____

x 5 ^{years} 240,000 f
96 assistants x 5 = 480 (+ 20. my 20 v.)
                         manuscript
           of the 480 cps.
                  not printed replaced by 500 f. hearing)
                         elicit ~~to 48,000 cps~~ 240000 cp.

SELECTED EXACT CHANGE TITLES

FOR A COMPLETE LIST PLEASE VISIT WWW.EXACTCHANGE.COM